Heteronormativity and Psychoanalysis

Heteronormativity and Psychoanalysis proposes a critical reading of the Freudian and Lacanian texts that paved the way for a heteronormative bias in the theory and practice of psychoanalysis.

Jorge N. Reitter's theoretical-political project engages in a genealogy of how psychoanalysis approached the 'gay question' through time. This book determinedly seeks to dismantle the heteronormative bias in the theories of psychoanalysis that resist new discourses on gender and sexuality. Drawing on developments by Michel Foucault and lesbian and gay studies on queer theory and feminist theorizing, Reitter draws attention to the normalizing devices that permanently regulate sexuality neglected by psychoanalysis as producers of subjectivities.

Accessibly written, *Heteronormativity and Psychoanalysis* will be key reading for psychoanalysts in practice and in training, as well as academics and students of psychoanalytic studies, gender studies, and sexualities.

Jorge N. Reitter is former teaching assistant in the Clinic for Adults, Faculty of Psychology at the University of Buenos Aires, Argentina. He is former Chair Professor of Sexuality and the Oedipus Complex at the Universidad Nacional Autónoma de Zacatecas, Mexico, and visiting professor at the Universidad de la República, Uruguay.

"Not just a compelling critique of the heteronormativity of institutionalized psychoanalysis, Jorge Reitter's book offers a bracing performative speech act whose effects will reverberate for some time to come. Out of the shadows emerges – if we dare to name it – a capaciously *queer* psychoanalysis for the twenty-first century".

Tim Dean, *James M. Benson Professor in English,*
University of Illinois at Urbana-Champaign; author of
Beyond Sexuality *and editor of* Homosexuality and
Psychoanalysis.

"Jorge Reitter is one of the present-day most innovative psychoanalysts in Argentina: his work is renowned among all Latin-America psychoanalysts, academics and students who wish to tackle minority gender and sexuality issues. The book very clearly sums up and analyses the main Freudian and Lacanian ambivalent stances on homosexuality and alternative sexualities, and suggests creative ways to renew psychoanalytic theory and practice. The book's main asset is to try and think of sexuality in terms of power relations, in a Foucauldian approach applied to psychoanalysis, yet from a psychoanalytic point of view".

Thamy Ayouch, *Psychoanalyst, Doctor of Research*
in Psychoanalysis (Université Paris 7), Maître de
Conférence (Full Professor) in Clinical Psychology
(Université Lille 3), Researcher and director of doctoral
research (Université Paris 7), Visiting Professor do
Exterior (Universidade de São Paulo), Former student
of Ecole Normale Supérieure.

"Jorge Reitter's book Edipo Gay is an important milestone for psychoanalysis as it is practiced in the 21st century. The book reconnects with the fundamental dimensions of clinical experience. However, it does so in a resolutely critical and open manner by purging both practice and theory of any risk of homophobic, transphobic or simply heteronormative conservatism. From a reflection on the so-called sexual minorities, Reitter manages to reinvent ethics at the heart of transferential dynamics and to assume the not only intimate but also political dimension of the analytic act".

Fabrice Bourlez is a psychoanalyst, doctor of philos-
ophy, he teaches at the esad in Reims, at SciencesPo
Paris and is co-holder of the Troubles, Dissidences and
Aesthetics chair at the Ecole Nationale Supérieure des
Beaux-Arts in Paris. He teaches psychoanalysis at the
International Institute of Psychoanalysis (Brazil). He
has written Pulsions Pasoliniennes (Presses du Réel,
2015) and Queer psychanalyse (Hermann, 2018).

"Jorge N. Reitter's book reminds us that psychoanalysis is first and foremost an act...here an act of writing where the author takes a position, as a psychoanalyst, in the scholarly public debate concerning minoritized sexualities and their conflicting relationships with the theories of Freud or Lacan, which are too often put at the service of a reactionary heteronormativity. As part of Freud's desire, Jorge N. Reitter thus revisits the Oedipus complex and the clinic of castration in the light of LGBTQIA+ approaches from – and this is perhaps the most important – arguments internal to our field".

Lionel Le Corre, psychoanalyst, researcher associated with the CRPMS, Université Paris Cité (France). Doctor in psychoanalytic anthropology. Author of the book Freud's Homosexuality.

"Reitter argues, and I agree with him, that psychoanalysis is not necessarily heteronormative, binary, and patriarchal. Psychoanalysis can do better things than it does by revising that matrix around its nodal concepts. Untying what was tied to conceptions of the time, with what is still sustained and keeps it vital and current. A necessary and avant-garde book that bets on a living psychoanalysis proposing a clinic of the specificity of the intrapsychic and the biopolitical of gay erotica and amorousness, both on the side of the patients and on the side of the analysts".

Débora Tajer, Feminist psychoanalyst and author of the book Psychoanalysis for Everyone. *Associate Professor in charge of the "Introduction to Gender Studies" Chair. Regular Associate Professor of the "Public Health/Mental Health II" Chair, Faculty of Psychology, UBA. Co-founder Forum of Psychoanalysis and Gender, Association of Psychologists of Buenos Aires.*

"Today the human is breaking with certain prohibitions and limits that were imposed on us a long time ago and in another history, and we do not allow ourselves to be determined externally (we emancipated ourselves with great rage from this); because the human is articulated with multiple pleasures that radically constitute it, with sexual diversities that flood it and complement it, and this is so because the logics of the world have changed, continue to change and cannot be stopped under any signifier Father. Jorge Nico Reitter expresses this becoming of each one of us in a brilliant and exemplary way in his book *Edipo Gay*. Moreover, Reitter, as the clinician that he is, knows it from the inside in the day today pain that the Other suffers in order to be accepted in this society of heteropatriarchal control; it is not only a question of the desire of this or that human being, but we are in the "Hegelian" dimension of the matter, namely, of the logics of power that allow or do not allow the performative and in this to speak of the diversity that we are and, in this, to feel accepted as such; for this reason his book becomes totally necessary for us to understand and transform our present".

Ricardo Espinosa Lolas Chilean writer, critical theorist and philosopher. Member of the Goldsmiths Center for Philosophy and Critical Thought. University of London.

"Jorge N. Reitter's book reminds us that psychoanalysis is first and foremost an act...here an act of writing where the author takes a position, as a psychoanalyst, in the scholarly public debate concerning minoritized sexualities and their conflicting relationships with the theories of Freud or Lacan, which are too often put at the service of a reactionary heteronormativity. As part of Freud's desire, Jorge N. Reitter thus revisits the Oedipus complex and the clinic of castration in the light of LGBTQIA+ approaches from – and this is perhaps the most important – arguments internal to our field".

Lionel Le Corre, psychoanalyst, researcher associated with the CRPMS, Université Paris Cité (France). Doctor in psychoanalytic anthropology. Author of the book Freud's Homosexuality.

"Jorge's text makes a vital intervention in spotlighting the challenges for the psychoanalytic field of remaining true to the unconscious as what precisely cannot be "normalised" and "mainstreamed." The text is a wake-up call to twenty-first century psychoanalysts to learn important lessons from its own history of (hetero)normalisation and to remain open to the heteros of the unconscious and to an ethics of subjectivity that is irreducible to any social classification or cultural appropriation".

Eve Watson, PhD. Psychoanalyst, Dublin, and Editor of Critical Essays on the Drive: Lacanian Theory and Practice *(2023).*

Heteronormativity and Psychoanalysis

Oedipus Gay

Jorge N. Reitter

Work published within the framework of "Sur" Translation Support Program of the Ministry of Foreign Affairs and Worship of the Argentine Republic

Obra editada en el marco del Programa "Sur" de Apoyo a las Traducciones del Ministerio de Relaciones Exteriores y Culto de la República Argentina

Routledge
Taylor & Francis Group

LONDON AND NEW YORK

Cover image: © Getty Images

First Edition published in Spanish as Edipo gay:
Heteronormatividad y psicoanálisis in 2018
by Letra Viva
Av. Coronel Díaz 1837, Buenos Aires, Argentina

Second Edition published in Spanish as Edipo gay:
Heteronormatividad y psicoanálisis in 2019
by Letra Viva
Av. Coronel Díaz 1837, Buenos Aires, Argentina

Work published within the framework of "Sur" Translation Support
Program of the Ministry of Foreign Affairs and Worship of the
Argentine Republic

Obra editada en el marco del Programa "Sur" de Apoyo a las
Traducciones del Ministerio de Relaciones Exteriores y Culto de la
República Argentina

First published in English in 2023
by Routledge
4 Park Square, Milton Park, Abingdon, Oxon OX14 4RN

and by Routledge
605 Third Avenue, New York, NY 10158

Routledge is an imprint of the Taylor & Francis Group, an informa business

© 2023 Jorge N. Reitter

British Library Cataloguing-in-Publication Data
A catalogue record for this book is available from the British Library

ISBN: 9781032171821 (hbk)
ISBN: 9781032171845 (pbk)
ISBN: 9781003252160 (ebk)

DOI: 10.4324/9781003252160

Typeset in Times New Roman
by codeMantra

To Sofía, to Alicia and to Olga
To the gay liberation movement

Contents

In the English edition

This English edition of *Heteronormativity and Psychoanalysis*, *Oedipus Gay*, has some differences from the second edition in Spanish. Translating it has given me the chance to correct some errors and update some points that I do not think exactly the same as in 2019. I removed a chapter that seems to me to be of no interest to English speakers since it discusses issues in Argentina. The most significant difference with respect to the previous edition is the inclusion of a new chapter, *Towards a post-heteronormative Oedipus*, which answers a question that readers of the book asked me on several occasions: if the Oedipus complex is the heteronormative deployment par excellence of psychoanalysis, why not discard it and aim, as many propose, toward a post-oedipal psychoanalysis? In that chapter, I give my answer.

There are countless people I would have to thank. I prefer to avoid naming all of them, because I am sure that no matter how exhaustive I try to be, someone will always be left out. There are, however, some people directly linked to this English edition whom I want to express my thanks.

First of all, Hugo Castaneda, the translator, who put his best effort toward this translation and had infinite patience with all my requests, doubts, and questions. To my editor, Susannah Frearson, who has treated me kindly since we met, has responded quickly and intelligently to all my concerns and questions and has been a fundamental support throughout the editing process. We have never met in person, and yet I feel close to her. My enormous thanks to Patricia Gherovici. Without her support, selfless generosity, and advice, this English version of the book would not have existed. It was she who encouraged me to present the book to the publisher and gave her support to the project. She was also our adviser on the questions that arose on the specific vocabulary of psychoanalysis when Hugo and I were in doubt about the most accurate translation.

I would also like to thank Diego Lorenzo and the Programa Sur de apoyo a las traducciones of the Dirección General de Asuntos Culturales de la Cancillería de la República Argentina, without whose help it would have been difficult to carry out the translation.

Finally, my thanks to the publisher, Routledge, for having deemed my book worthy enough to be printed in English.

Buenos Aires
April 2022

Prologue by Patricia Gherovici

I was fortunate to meet and befriend the late literary scholar, theorist, and brilliant critic Leo Bersani, who often engaged with psychoanalytic theory in his writings. In what remains his most famous essay, the 1987 "Is the Rectum a Grave?", Bersani wrote about sexuality and gay identity during the height of the AIDS crisis. A few years ago, we had a conversation in a café in Philadelphia, during which he shared how painful his experience of psychoanalytic treatment had been. He was a young man then and had an analyst who was fixated on curing his homosexuality. Caught in the slippery terrain of transferential mutual implication, Bersani was torn between his analyst's wish and his own desires. As a psychoanalyst, I was appalled and ashamed to hear this; however, this did not surprise me so much, for I had heard similar stories. In the rest of our conversation, and I am not sure whether this is an accurate recollection or a wishful distortion, my memory has retained the fact that Bersani confided that his psychoanalyst eventually turned a corner and realized that he was wasting his time. However, I can take full responsibility for the legacy left by misguided psychoanalysts who were intent on "curing" homosexuality. Today we have learned that it is homophobia, not homosexuality, that is the cause of the suffering experienced by people like Leo Bersani. If this book had been published a few decades ago, Bersani's analyst might have read Jorge N. Reitter's critique of psychoanalysis' heterosexism, and embraced erotic desire in all its polymorphous potential, rather than fall into oppressive strategies to assuage anxieties and, perhaps, as Michel Foucault would have argued, to silence the revolutionary political potential of gayness.

It is undeniable that for many years homosexuality was considered to be a pathology in psychoanalytic circles, even though the founder of psychoanalysis, Sigmund Freud himself, never condemned it. Freud had a tolerant attitude. He never considered same-sex desire as pathological, because for him homosexuality was a sexual orientation like any other: it was as contingent as heterosexuality. Freud observed "that all human beings are capable of making a homosexual object-choice and have in fact made one in their unconscious" (1905, 145n.)[1] But until the 1990s, traditional psychoanalysis thought that homosexuality was deviant, a perversion. Whereas the American Psychiatric Association, under the pressure of gay activists, decreed in 1973 that homosexuality was not a mental disorder, psychoanalysts continued to consider homosexuality as a pathology for another 30 years. Only in

1991 did psychoanalytic training institutes adopt a policy prohibiting discrimination on the basis of sexual orientation.

In clinical practice in the United States, psychoanalysis remained very close to psychiatry until the late 1980s. Moreover, between the 1930s and 1980s, only medically trained psychiatrists could be accepted as candidates or members of the American Psychoanalytic Association (APsaA). In 1987, APsaA finally agreed to admit psychologists and social workers for analytic training.

In 1973, when homosexuality was still considered as a mental illness, a "sociopathic personality disturbance" according to the so-called Bible of psychiatric diagnosis, the American Psychiatric Association's (APA) Diagnostic and Statistical Manual of Mental Disorders, something strange happened. A disquieting-looking Dr Henry Anonymous, who was a psychiatrist wearing an oversized tuxedo, a disheveled wig, and a scary rubber face mask that curiously anticipated the notorious "leather-face" popularized by the horror movie "The Texas Chainsaw Massacre" one year later, and who used a voice distorting microphone to protect his identity and his career, spoke at the APA annual meeting, presenting himself saying: "I am a homosexual. I am a psychiatrist". Dr Anonymous argued that his colleagues should eliminate homosexuality as a mental disorder; he pleaded with them to end horrible treatments such as chemical castration, electric shock therapy, and lobotomy. His appeal convinced psychiatrists who actually declassified homosexuality as a mental disorder.

Despite this, it took American psychoanalysts another 20 years to stop considering homosexuality as a pathology. It was under threat of an anti-discrimination lawsuit that only in 1991 allowed the training of gay and lesbian psychoanalysts. Later on, the American Psychoanalytic Association (APsaA) went on to become a supporter of same-sex marriage, also opposing the practice of "conversion therapy" aimed at changing a person's sexual orientation. Finally, in June of 2019, during Gay Pride month, The American Psychoanalytic Association (APsaA) publicly apologized for previously treating homosexuality as a mental illness, and admitted that its past errors had contributed to discrimination and trauma for LGBTQIA+ people.

The normative tendency in psychoanalysis contradicted the original Freudian spirit. Freud's well-known 1935 letter to the American mother of a gay man made it clear that there was nothing wrong with being homosexual. "I gather from your letter that your son is a homosexual. I am most impressed by the fact that you do not mention this term for yourself in your information about him. May I question you why you avoid it?", he wrote.

> Homosexuality is assuredly no advantage, but it is nothing to be ashamed of, no vice, no degradation; it cannot be classified as an illness; we consider it to be a variation of the sexual function. . . . Many highly respectable individuals of ancient and modern times have been homosexuals, several of the greatest men among them.[2]

Freud added that persecuting homosexuality constituted "a crime and cruelty too", thus reiterating the unequivocal opinion he had expressed three decades earlier in a 1903 interview in the Viennese newspaper *Die Zeit* when a prominent man was on trial for homosexuality: "Homosexual people are not sick, but they also do not belong in a court of law". Why penalize homosexuality since in terms of psychic unconscious dynamics this is just a variation of the sexual function that is as inexplicable as heterosexuality? On the whole, Freud acknowledged that heterosexuality or the attraction between men and women is not a norm but rather "a problem that needs elucidating and is not a self-evident fact".[3] Homosexuality was as mysterious and problematic as heterosexuality. Nevertheless, post-Freudian psychoanalysts have talked about "normal" sexuality, assuming that it means heterosexual genital function.

As Jacques Lacan observed, Freud posited human "sexuality as essentially polymorphous, aberrant" (1981). Freud created an outrage with his early sexual theories, not merely with the claim that children were sexual beings but also with his non-essentialism in his definition of sexuality. Freud's later notion of the drive is also non–gender-specific. This revelation would clash with hetero-normative sensibilities, and it was thereafter repressed by post-Freudians. Indeed, Freud "perverted" sexuality when he separated the drive from any instinctual function and described its object as "indifferent", that is, not determined by gender. Freud forces us to think differently then, if contrary to the standard view of traditional psychoanalysis, Freud had "queered" human sexuality, as Tim Dean and Christopher Lane argue, and proposed a sexuality that operates in a mysterious, capricious way, *contra naturam*, veering off the reproductive aims.

Freud used the story of Oedipus to invent a theory that would solve the problem of sexuality. In this book, Reitter points to the problems of the Oedipus complex as an unsatisfactory resolution if applied mechanically, in a "generic" manner; he offers new postulates that rescue Oedipus from the "norm" and makes room for sexual diversity so as to transform the contemporary clinic.

Since 2018, Reitter has been showing that although both Freud and Lacan's theories may provide a structure that challenges any construction of normativity, how Lacanian psychoanalysis is practiced and transmitted today, even with psychoanalysts who do not consider themselves homophobic, continues to support compulsory heterosexuality in explicit and implicit ways. We find echoes of this criticism of psychoanalytic discourse and practices in a recent public event that took place on November 17, 2019. The speaker was not wearing a creepy rubber mask like Dr. Anonymous, but rather the metaphorical disguise of an ape. This is how the philosopher and trans-activist Paul B. Preciado spoke to an annual gathering of Lacanian psychoanalysts in Paris who, like the 1970s APA psychiatrists, still appear to believe in heterosexual normativity.[4] Controversy was triggered by the very first opening words when Preciado addressed the audience of 3,500 psychoanalysts with the customary greeting "ladies and gentlemen" and extended his greeting to those who were neither ladies nor gentlemen. Preciado pointedly asked whether there was at least one psychoanalyst in the huge auditorium who was openly queer, trans, or non-binary. The response was a glacial silence interrupted by nervous giggles. He continued by asking whether any of the psychoanalytic institutions present at the meeting assumed any responsibility for the current changes in what he called the "epistemology of gender and sexuality", that is, the way we think, talk, and theorize about gender and sexuality, as well as an acknowledgment of the limits of what we know. The audience was divided between those who cheered and those who booed and demanded that Preciado leave the premises.

His presentation was captured by many portable phone cameras, and the recorded video became as viral as a leaked sex tape, sending waves across the psychoanalytic world. Just a few days later, provisional transcriptions of the lecture were circulated, translated into Spanish, Italian, and English and quickly published online. Several approximate versions of the lecture appeared in Argentina, Colombia, Germany, Spain, Brazil, and France. In response to this unauthorized circulation of his lecture, Preciado published the full original text in a short book that appeared in 2020 in French, Spanish, and English under the title *Can the Monster Speak? Report to the Academy of Psychoanalysts.*

Preciado was wittily alluding to Franz Kafka's 1917 short story "Report to an Academy". In the story, an ape named Red Peter, who has learned to behave like a human, presents to an academy of experts the story of how he achieved his transformation into an acceptable educated European (but he is ready to pull his pants down whenever he needs to show a bullet wound commemorating his capture in the African Gold Coast). Thus, Preciado exhibited himself as a transsexual specimen like Kafka's ape, who ironically claimed that he was as "human" as anyone in the audience, the product of a deliberate transformation. For his speech in 2019, Preciado chose to quote Kafka's fable of an educated ape who stands before the members of a learned society telling the story of his life, not unlike the brave gesture of Dr. Anonymous in 1973, not as a story of emancipation but rather as "a critique of colonial European humanism and its anthropological categories". Paul became a monkey transformed into a human to escape the confines of his cage. Preciado told the audience:

> Just as the monkey Red Peter, so today I address myself to you, the academicians of psychoanalysis, from my 'cage' as a transsexual man. I, a body marked by medical and juridical discourse as 'transsexual,' characterized by most of your psychoanalytic diagnoses as a subject of an 'unthinkable metamorphosis' find myself, according to most of your theories, beyond neurosis, on the cusp of—or perhaps even within the bounds of—psychosis, being incapable, according to you, of correctly resolving an Oedipus complex, or having succumbed to penis envy.

Preciado continued, "I address you, an ape-human in a new era. The monster you have created with your discourse and clinical practices". ... "As a trans body, as a non-binary body whose right to speak as an expert about my condition"... "I have done as Peter the Red did, I learnt the language of Freud and Lacan, the language of the colonial patriarchy, your language and I am here to address you". He explained that while he turned to Kafka's story, the theme of the 2019 symposium "Women in Psychoanalysis" seemed closer to the era of the author of the *Metamorphosis* than to our own. He criticized the organizers of the conference for talking about women in psychoanalysis as if they were exotic animals, not yet fully recognized as political subjects, and suggested that "it might have been better to organize an event on the subject of white heterosexual middle-class men in psychoanalysis" (20). Preciado's lecture addressed the heteronormativity and binarism of psychoanalysis, that is, the sad tradition in psychoanalysis, Lacanian and otherwise, of pathologizing any non-normative expression of gender or sexuality, a tradition that Reitter had criticized since the 2018 publication of *Edipo Gay: Heteronormatividad y psicoanálisis.*

The present book challenges the psychoanalytic tradition of considering the heterosexual, genital, reproductive, family-oriented inclination as a norm, a model where any deviation from this pattern will be pathologized. This reconsideration is overdue. For instance, even in Freud, it is expected that any female subject will have to move her center of erotic enjoyment from the clitoris to the vagina in order to achieve full reproductive maturity. Freud infamously compared the issue of female sexuality to the dark continent of Africa.

Reitter's book is a timely wake-up call. Because I agree with Reitter's historical reframing, I will share with you one important but forgotten chapter in the history of psychoanalysis of a non-binary, non-normative ideology outside the epistemology Preciado criticizes. I will go back to the early days of psychoanalysis when Freud collaborated with the leading sexologists of his time. Among them was Magnus Hirschfeld, the so-called Dr Einstein of sex, founder of the world's first sexual research institute in Berlin, and pioneering researcher, clinician, and LGBT advocate who did groundbreaking work on transgenderism, publishing more than 2,000 articles on homosexuality and sexually variant behaviors. Hirschfeld, a passionate sex reformer and an activist, was also an occasional cross-dresser and a central political figure in Germany's incipient field of sexology. He published a number of early psychoanalytic papers, including that of Freud.

Hirschfeld played a central role in the early days of psychoanalysis.[5] Freud and Hirschfeld collaborated closely: Freud contributed articles to his journals while Hirschfeld took a serious interest in psychoanalysis. Furthermore, Hirschfeld co-founded the Berlin Psychoanalytic Society with Karl Abraham in August 1908. In 1911, at the third international congress of psychoanalysts, Freud greeted Hirschfeld very warmly as an honored guest and publicly expressed his admiration for "the Berlin authority on homosexuality". Yet even with this recognition, Hirschfeld left the Berlin Psychoanalytic Society shortly after the Weimar meeting, despite Abraham's attempts to persuade him to stay.

Hirschfeld's departure had been precipitated by "an external cause", also described by Abraham as "a question of resistances" when Jung objected to his homosexuality. Unlike Jung, Freud saw Hirschfeld's advocacy of homosexual rights as a positive development and from the beginning encouraged Abraham to work with him. Hirschfeld's departure deeply embittered Freud but he hid his disappointment by commenting that this was not such a huge loss. However, not long before the split, Freud wrote to Jung expressing his wish to include sexologists in the psychoanalytic movement and insisted on the importance of such a collaboration.

While Freud and Hirschfeld both opposed the criminalization of same-sex desire and did not consider it an abnormality in the pathological sense, they disagreed about what caused homosexuality. Hirschfeld believed in biological, inborn homosexuality while Freud considered that childhood experiences determined unconscious libidinal tendencies and object choices. Rather than advocating against the punishment of non-normative sexual manifestations based on the claim that biological variations determinate behavior, Freud's original approach was to separate sex from reproduction by highlighting the skewed character of human sexuality. One can read Freud in a normative, patriarchal manner and associate masculinity with activity and femininity with passivity, emphasizing penis envy, female masochism, and the role of the father, but one can also find a "Pink Freud".

In a foundational psychoanalytic text of 1905, *Three Essays on Sexuality*, Freud (1953b) conceives of the sexual drive as fundamentally bisexual and intrinsically queer, as Christopher Lane and Tim Dean (2001) have shown. Philippe Van Haute and Herman Westerink (2017) have demonstrated in a careful textual study that Freud's first edition of the *Three Essays* did not mention the Oedipus complex and promoted a de-heterosexual and polymorphous sexuality. Such a "queerness" of psychoanalysis has been productively elaborated upon in the work of Judith Butler (1990), David Eng (2001), Lee Edelman (2004), and Preciado (2008), among others.

Using the critical tools of psychoanalysis, queer studies showed that at the level of the sexual drive there is no predetermined object or gender, and consequently, no prescriptive norm. The potential freedom of the sexual drive, a freedom which is also its doom, does not sit well with the public, or even with most psychoanalysts, as we have seen. Psychoanalysis tended to address this reality through the lens of conservative values. This goes against the grain of psychoanalysis' own foundations, as its theory has been at the root of many trenchant critiques of the dominant hetero-patriarchal culture.

While Freud never grappled with gender directly, he problematized human sexuality when he defined sexual difference as the psychical consequence of the child's discovery of the anatomical distinction between the sexes. Even though Freud's work on infantile sexuality appears to describe a progression from childhood latency to adult sexual activity, he nevertheless proposes a nonlinear evolution, as is made clear by even the most cursory reading of his famous case studies. Insofar as it denaturalizes sex in terms of culture and history and problematizes gender as unstable and conflicted, psychoanalysis offers us the tools to reconsider patriarchal and heterosexist forms of cultural and ideological domination. This is precisely what Reitter does in this crisp, intelligent, and highly readable book.

The story by Kafka that Preciado evoked in his 2019 speech goes beyond a meditation of the human-animal divide. It also touches on issues of race and colonialism. While Red Ape cannot remember his past animal life any longer, in the "civilized life" his "race" is not held against him, rather he is showered with attention and even admiration. His "racial" heredity is not an obstacle but quite the opposite – his efforts at becoming human are appreciated, even loved, precisely because he is an ape, a member of an alien species (Walter Sokel, 2002, 266). In an imperialist gesture, a native of Africa is captured, slaved, and imported to Europe. A reversed frame but a similar survivalist wish for assimilation was experienced by the psychoanalysts who undertook a forced migration to the United States to escape Nazi persecution before the Second World War. Can we say that they engaged in a failed attempt at decolonization? That first decolonization was a failure because they were trying to make psychoanalysis less European by medicalizing the practice. This Americanizing of the unconscious erased sexuality and any political dimension and also assumed that psychoanalysis was outside history.

Perhaps a new mode of decolonization is needed now. New decolonization of psychoanalysis would not focus so much on adaptation or consensus but dissensus, as the philosopher Jacques Rancière (1995/2010) proposed. The idea of dissensus was also discussed in 1995 by the Franco-Egyptian psychoanalyst Jacques Hassoun. Dissensus is a mingling of contradictory or divergent opinions, literally dis-sensus, meaning a process of reordering. Dissensus may not come naturally; it may be something we need to practice before we can learn it. Dissensus is the exact opposite of consensus. For Rancière, politics is not a matter of institutions or social arrangements, but instead a matter of what people do, and, in particular, of people's power to disrupt. Hopefully, disruption will lead to a more just social arrangement. Often, we believe that consensus is good and dissensus is bad, but one may forget that disagreement is needed for change to occur. As we know, democracy relies on dissensus as much as on consensus.

Today, to pursue my dissensus, I want to imagine a different future for psychoanalysis, a future that acknowledges its past errors in order to move forward. To accomplish this, the reader will need to follow Reitter's carefully etched argument that makes us aware of the dehumanizing consequences of psychoanalytic prejudice. Reitter proposes a non-heteronormative theory of the practice challenging the use in hegemonic psychoanalysis of the Oedipus complex and the castration complex to impose heteronormativity. Reiter writes as a gay analyst, speaking from what has been historically a marginalized position. Beyond this, he also writes as a psychoanalyst, which means that he upholds an ethical position of desire for difference.

In 1972, Gilles Deleuze and Felix Guattari shook the psychoanalytic establishment with their *Anti-Oedipus: Capitalism and Schizophrenia*, a book that attacked the normative use of the Oedipal structure that they saw dominating after Freud. Today, half a century later, Reitter gives us an *Oedipus Gay* to show the other side of Freud and psychoanalysis and offer a radically non-heteronormative vision of sexual diversity. His gay Oedipus takes off his mask and reveals that he is one with Dr Anonymous.

Works Cited

Bersani, L. (1987). Is the rectum a grave? In D. Crimp (Ed.), *AIDS: Cultural analysis/cultural activism* (Vol. 43, pp. 197–222). Boston, MA: MIT Press.

Butler, J. (1990). *Gender trouble: Feminism and the subversion of identity.* New York, NY: Routledge.

Dean, T., & Lane, C. (Eds.). (2001). *Homosexuality and psychoanalysis.* Chicago, IL: University of Chicago Press.

Deleuze, G., & Guattari, F. (2004). *Anti-oedipus: Capitalism and schizophrenia.* London and New York, NY: Continuum.

Dose, R. (2014). *Magnus Hirschfeld: The origins of the gay liberation movement.* New York, NY: Monthly Review Press.

Edelman, L. (2005). *No future: Queer theory and the death drive.* Durham, NC: Duke University Press.

Eng, D. (2001). *Racial castration: Managing masculinity in Asian America.* Durham, NC: Duke University Press.

Freud, S. (1953). Three essays on the theory of sexuality (1905). In J. Strachey (Ed.), *The standard edition of the complete psychological works of Sigmund Freud.* (J. Strachey, Trans) (Vol. 7, pp. 123–146). London: Hogarth Press.

Freud, S. (1960). Anonymous (Letter to an American Mother). In E. Freud (Ed.), *The letters of Sigmund Freud* (pp. 423–424). London: Hogarth Press.

Gherovici, P. (2017). *Transgender psychoanalysis: A Lacanian perspective on sexual difference.* New York, NY: Routledge.

Lacan, J. (1981). *The seminar of Jacques Lacan: The four fundamental concepts of psychoanalysis.* (J.-A. Miller, Ed.; A. Sheridan, Trans.). New York, NY: W.W. Norton & Company.

Mancini, E. (2010). *Magnus Hirschfeld and the quest for sexual freedom.* New York, NY: Palgrave.

Preciado, P. B. (2008). *Testo Junkie: Sex, drugs, and biopolitics in the pharmacopornographic era.* (B. Benderson, Trans.). New York, NY: The Feminist Press.

Preciado, P. B. (2021). *Can the monster speak? Report to the academy of psychoanalysts.* Semiotext(e)/Intervention Series. Los Angeles, CA: Semiotext(e) Intervention Series.

Rancière, J. (2010). *Dinssensus: On politics and aesthetics.* New York, NY: Continuum.

Sokel, W. H. (2002). *The myth of power and the self: Essays on Franz Kafka.* Detroit: Wayne State University Press.

Van Haute, P., & Westerink, H. (2017). *Desconstructing normativity? Re-reading Freud's 1905 three essays.* New York, NY: Routledge.

Prologue to the First Edition

Homophobia in the closet

On the first of December 1921, Ernst Jones mentions, in one of the circular letters of the Secret Committee, that the Dutch consulted him on the advisability of accepting "a doctor known openly as a homosexual" (Wittenberger and Tögel, 2002, 204) as a member of the psychoanalytic society. Jones discourages them and raises the question to the remaining committee members of whether the exclusion of homosexuals from analytic training should be the general norm for the International Psychoanalytic Association (I.P.A.). Freud and Rank disagree, arguing that "the decision in such cases should be based on an individual assessment of the qualities of the person". (201) To my disappointment, the position of Ferenczi (who, prior to his encounter with psychoanalysis had valiantly defended the rights of "Uranists" before the Budapest Medical Association) is that "for the moment, it would be better to reject all open homosexuals on principle; they are generally too abnormal". (213) Finally, the position of denying homosexuals the possibility of receiving psychoanalytic training triumphs, without Freud having opposed this decision with the firmness with which he defended the "lay" analysis.

This position prevailed in the I.P.A. for more than 50 years, but *it was never put in writing*. In the United States, and by the effort and struggle of the gay liberation movement itself, things started to change. In France, Jacques Lacan was, at the clinical and institutional level, the first to radically break off from the persecution of homosexuals in the I.P.A. He analyzed them without trying to "cure" them of their homosexuality and never prevented them from becoming analysts if they desired. According to Elisabeth Roudinesco, when Lacan founded the École Freudienne de Paris in 1964, "he accepted the principle of their integration as training analysts". However, on a theoretical level, he never failed to place homosexuality on the side of perversion.

I do not have the impression that this liberality in the acts of Lacan has carried over to the Lacanian institutions. I remember, for example, that in my years as a student at the School of Psychology at the University of Buenos Aires (a school that was experiencing a Lacanian euphoria in that post-dictatorship climate), the question was raised whether a homosexual, a "perverse" according to Lacan, could be a psychoanalyst. It has been several years since then, but only a couple of days ago, they were telling me that Jorge Alemán[6] had asked, in a seminar, which psychoanalytic society would allow members to be openly gay.

When the militants of the Gay Liberation Front fought with the American Psychiatric Association to remove homosexuality from the *Diagnostic and Statistical Manual of Mental Disorders*, they raised the proposal: "stop talking *about* us, talk *to* us". That was already trying to destabilize power relations: do not treat us as objects, we are subjects. However, this ran the risk of establishing that the psychiatrists were on one side, gays on the other when obviously there were many psychiatrists who were also gay (in that context, very much in the closet). In the conference that decided on the elimination of homosexuality as a pathology, it was sought, as a political measure that a psychiatrist who was also gay, will attempt to prevent the field of psychiatry (for that matter, the scientific field) from becoming heterosexual. I doubt that this deconstruction has yet occurred in our psychoanalytic institutions.

Throughout the chapters, I incur some reiterations that I would have liked to avoid. But in the editing process, I became aware that a fair share of what I propose is based on things *not written*. In fact, psychoanalytic literature on homosexuality, or if we prefer, on gayness, is almost non-existent in recent decades. I had to make use, to a large extent, of things I hear (or that others tell me that someone heard) in a seminar, a study group (but always as an aside, something said as in parentheses), phrases said in the corridors of a conference, in interventions in analyses that are presented to me after prior analyses, or through inquiries which are made to me after reading a text of mine or watching a video online.[7] I cannot help recalling here the things said but never written down that Freud hears from three of his teachers about the sexual etiology of hysteria. The reiterations that I could not avoid, I understood were not only due to my limitations but also to the very limited material *written* on the subject. Why is the relationship between psychoanalysis and homosexuality not written about or just mentioned only in the margins? It seems that the "epistemology of the closet" (Kosofsky Sedgwick) governs the relations between psychoanalysis and gayness in the last few decades.[8] Throughout these pages, I attempt to unravel, in various theorizations of psychoanalysis, some of the reasons for this difficulty, which has affected and continues to affect negatively the lives of many people.

The order of the chapters in the first part is chronological. The first version of the first chapter is from 2013, the last from 2017. Some ideas are inevitably repeated because I stubbornly search for answers to the same question: can less heteronormative ways be found to pose the relationship between the Oedipus complex and the castration complex (as I intend to demonstrate in this book, the heteronormative *dispositif par excellence* of psychoanalysis)? I believe, as the chapters progress, that my ideas gain more precision, although there is still a long way to go. The second part brings together a miscellany of short articles of various topics, but always related to the main topic. Finally, as a sort of *bonus track*, there is a conversation with

Manuel Murillo and Pablo Tajman, in which I feel that I managed to express my ideas clearly, with the added freshness that dialogue with others gives.

Theoretical production in psychoanalysis does not usually arise from pure and disinterested science (if any science is): it includes the subject and their desire. This book is the journey, the product, and the testimony of a sustained and intense subjective work (and painful grief) to solve matters which no psychoanalysis could solve. For this reason, while most of what is written are transferable to other forms of sexual diversity, this book is especially focused on the matter of male gayness.

Notes

1 Sigmund Freud, "Three Essays on the Theory of Sexuality (1905)", in *The Standard Edition of the Complete Psychological Works of Sigmund Freud*, vol. 7, ed. and trans. James Strachey (London: Hogarth Press, 1960). Footnote added in 1915; 145n.
2 Sigmund Freud, "Anonymous (Letter to an American Mother)", in E. Freud, ed., *The Letters of Sigmund Freud*, 423–424 (London: Hogarth Press, 1960).
3 Sigmund Freud, "Three Essays of the Theory of Sexuality", footnote added in 1915, 146n.
4 On November 17, 2019, Paul Preciado spoke at the École de la Cause Freudienne annual conference. The meeting was on the theme "Women in Psychoanalysis" and was convoked with an opaque description full of perplexing observations such as "In psychoanalysis, there are women!". This is probably why the organizers wanted as a keynote speaker a notorious female to male trans figure.
5 For more on Hirschfeld and psychoanalysis, see Gherovici, P. *Transgender Psychoanalysis* (2017), 44–46.
6 Well-known Argentine psychoanalyst who resides in Spain.
7 Since I began to spread the message of this book, a good amount of gay people from different places have reached out to me with doubts regarding the positions of their psychoanalysts. They suspected a heteronormative pressure in their analysis, but, as a result of the transference, they could not bring themselves to believe it. I must say that most of the time the suspicion was completely justified.
8 Prior to Stonewall, there was an abundance of psychoanalytic literature on homosexuality considered as a pathology.

I

Heteronormativity and psychoanalysis

1 Oedipus gay

This book arises from the conviction, surely controversial, that hegemonic[1] psychoanalysis *"as it is practiced"* does not mesh well with sexualities that do not respond well to heterosexual normativity. Of course, there are many ways to differ from the heterosexual norm, and each one requires a particular treatment. I am going to focus on some aspects of the relationship of psychoanalysis with male "homosexuality",[2] the form of sexuality that shows that the masters also have a hole that potentially harbors *jouissance*.

Of course, "psychoanalysis" is a very complex field, not at all homogeneous. There are theorizations from psychoanalysis that strongly challenge heteronormativity, and analysts, even in hegemonic institutions, are much more willing than others to embrace other forms of sexuality, just as there are those who pride themselves on "curing homosexuals", who then are considered sick. Although, my conviction is that beyond all these important differences, personal sympathies or antipathies, politically correct positions, genuine acceptances or eloquent silences, psychoanalysis *as it is practiced and transmitted* remains, in some of its hegemonic conceptualizations, on the side of the apparatus for the regulation of compulsory heterosexuality.

My statement will be controversial for at least two reasons. First, there will be those who do not agree with my opinion, those who believe that psychoanalysis does not have any prejudice with respect to other forms of sexuality. It will also be controversial in the sense that they will contend that there is nothing specific about the gay experience, that this is not a category of psychoanalysis, and therefore, not a pertinent topic.[3] Regarding the gay experience, my impression is that psychoanalysis tends to be in one of two positions (sometimes the same analyst holds both!): Either "homosexuality" is a pathology, or it is not an issue.[4] Although I agree that gay, or "homosexual", are not categories of psychoanalysis, I believe that there is a specificity of the gay experience, which a psychoanalyst must take into account when listening to a homosexual person. By "gay experience", I mean the one that someone goes through just because they are gay, regardless of all other subjective considerations. The two major manifestations of that experience are the insult and the closet, with the counterpart of the complex and, many times, precarious coming out of the closet. A gay person can stay in the

DOI: 10.4324/9781003252160-2

closet their whole life, another can come out of the closet in certain spaces, but not in others, and another can say – let them think what they want, I am not hiding. Those are the unique differences, but everyone, *by virtue of being gay* (and for this no consideration of "clinical structure" accounts), knows the experience of the closet and, whether they want to or not, continuously has to make decisions about it. In the same way, every gay person, whether they are really insulted or not, must count, *because they are gay*, with the possibility of insult – a threat that will always be on the horizon.

If the analyst does not understand the specificity of that experience and does not understand that it is not attributable to that particular subject, but to the position that the gay subject has concerning the Other (an Other that includes much more than language or parents, that includes the educational system, the media, the State, the medical-psychiatric and legal discourse, artistic representations – a very complex and, fortunately, not always coherent power structure), it is almost certain that the power relations which escape their understanding (and possibly that of their analysand) will be projected onto the analysand as if they were subjective. In this way, the most probable outcome is that instead of helping to solve the neurosis, they will generate more guilt and repression.

Freud posits a relationship between homosexuality and paranoia. We, homosexuals, are a bit paranoid, it seems. It is true, except that "paranoia" cannot be reduced to "psychological" mechanisms; they are the power devices sustaining compulsory heterosexuality that so frequently generate a "paranoid" response. A gay person does not *feel*[5] persecuted for their gayness – in many situations they *are*; it is not, or it is *not just*, a neurotic fantasy. If we think about it only in terms of "psychological" mechanisms, we only reinforce the power *dispositifs* that impose silence on the topic. We will be telling the subject that *they* have a problem when the problem is larger and more complex than a persecutory fantasy. I am not saying that persecutory fantasies do not exist, but we must also question how they are produced.

Frequently, in my discussions with some of my colleagues, we reach a disagreement that will surely not have a resolution, and which may not need one; it might be that we have different ways of reading this point. They accuse me of confusing subjective causes with social ones; I reproach them for taking too little into account the enormous dependence of the subject on the Other.[6] They, from my point of view, reduce everything to a certain conception of the subject that, in so doing, comes dangerously close to the individual. I have no doubt that we must focus on the subject, but I keep in mind that there is no subject without the Other and that starting from the Other there is a subject.

Sometimes, it seems to me my colleagues believe the only thing that counts is singularity – the famous *case-by-case basis*, which is undoubtedly fundamental, but only makes sense in its dialectic relationship with the general.[7] According to my point of view, if we do not take into account the dependence that the subject has on the Other, we can imperceptibly generate the idea of a certain omnipotence of the subject, which would not depend on certain historical-social conditions or on the network of power relations.[8] I want to be very clear on this point: I am not referring to a subject that is formed in a family, in an oedipal context, and after encounters, certain historical-social conditions and certain power relations. What I am saying is that those conditions and relationships make the subject who they truly are. These conditions and relationships are already present in the language that surrounds the subject and in the family in which the subject will develop their own oedipal drama. They also set very determined limits to constitute oneself as a subject.[9] Perhaps, with great subjective work, the subject can make a difference, become an agent of their own discourse, state their own truth, and give an answer. Then, their uniqueness will flourish, and we can think about the subject on a case-by-case basis.

The very fact of being the subject of *language* implies dependence: on the discourses that precede the subject, place them in a certain role, and set limits that they may or may not transgress, but that possibility of transgressing is dependent on determinations that always make the subject, a situated subject. As a crucial point in my argument, *power relations are immanent to language from the start: there is no language that is outside of them.*

It seems to me that there are certain conditions in which it is *apparently* possible to disregard a certain reading of the power devices that constitute the subject; this is when we share with the other, our neighbor, many factors, which include: class, race, nationality, sexuality, etc. In that case, the fact of not reading the position of the Other, of being only attentive to the fantasized aspect of the relationship to the Other, may not make a great obstacle to the development of a treatment, although, in any case, there is a risk of naturalizing what is actually constructed, historical, and contingent.

I will put it in these terms as well: in each context of class, race, gender, and sexual orientation, the signifiers are combined in such a way that the words, the phrases, take on more or less established meanings.[10] Of course, that will not prevent a subject from making their own combinations, but it will be based on those consensual and established senses. For example, the word *fag* is going to be uttered in a completely different manner in macho speech as an insult than when used by two gay men to address each other, giving it the value of a "decontextualized citation of an insult" or, as Judith Butler[11] calls it, a form of "performative inversion".

However, insofar as it is about interacting with another person with whom, in some of the aforementioned aspects or others, we do not share a similar position concerning the Other (when the place we occupy in power relations is very different), we run a serious risk of projecting our prejudices (of class, race, gender, etc.) if we do not take power relations into account when listening. For example, when listening to an analysand from a social class different from ours, we always run the risk of attributing to their subjectivity, in terms of their singular response, that which is attributable to the class modes of that subject, in the sense that these modes do not define any of the analysand's uniqueness. As analysts, and especially in some circumstances, we have to be a bit like anthropologists.

We also have to be a bit of a historian. History is one of the royal ways for the castration of the Other. For example, when children begin to understand that parents were also children – that they also had parents and had to deal with issues similar to those that occupy them – that is when they locate a dimension of the story; they can de-idealize the parents, humanize them, and castrate them. To contextualize the gay experience at this moment in the culture of some Western countries, we will take a very brief tour of some milestones – chosen based on activism, militancy, that is, the act of speaking up and fighting to alter power relations – trying to thread the place (contradictory, as we will see) that psychoanalysis occupied in that plot.

Theologians, psychiatrists, and activists

In what is referred to as the gay experience, there is something to which we analysts should, I think, be very sensitive: enunciation, the possibility of speaking, and the obligation to remain silent. It is not at all by chance that this text began with an epigraph by Foucault about the strategic role of silence. In the Christian West (leaving Greco-Roman antiquity aside) the *only* testimonies of the then "sodomy" that we have prior to the mid-nineteenth century are those of the inquisitors, theologians, and judges. Until the 1860s, when the first voices began to be heard, "homosexuality", which still used other names to call itself, had not been spoken of in the first person. If everything could be reduced to matters related to the subject, to their desire, to a subject that is thus reduced to the individual, if it were to reach an approach based on the "case-by-case", as if each one could do what they want in absolute terms (not determined), why did no one speak for such a long period of time and, then, the voices multiply rapidly? It is evident that a change in historical circumstances (read, in power relations) *made it possible* to speak. Sure, in theory, nothing would prevent someone in the sixteenth century from, for example, speaking up to defend love between men. However, if talking can cost you torture and a trip to the stake, you will think twice. We thus see the close relationship between discourse and power, a relationship that, when enjoying places of power (being bourgeois, being white, being heterosexual, being cis), is much easier to overlook. Yet, it seems clear to me that if speaking is going to cost you your life, or the loss of everything that gives it meaning and affords it a place in society, silence is imposed. Let us then differentiate staying silent, as an act of the subject, from *having to be silent*, as a determination external to the subject. Moreover, as analysts, we know to what extent, for a subject, being silent, or being silenced, implies not actualizing oneself.

One of the distant starting points of this injunction to silence the erotic desires between men in the framework of Christianity is the medieval reading of the epistle of Saint Paul to the Ephesians. Just to be clear, these are things to which, as analysts, we must pay close attention; the starting point *is not* the epistle of the inventor of Christianity, but the medieval reading of a passage from it. In verse 3 of Chapter 5, Saint Paul says: "But fornication, and all uncleanness, or covetousness, let it not be once named among you, as becometh saints" presumably meaning – you should not do such things, and you should not even speak of them. Some medieval theologians read this passage as the existence of a sin so grave that just naming it was infamous, and they decided, for very complex reasons that I cannot dwell upon in the context of this work, that this sin was precisely … sodomy. It is clear that the epistle of Saint Paul does not even state sodomy, but that is how the passage was interpreted, bringing, of course, enormous consequences.[12] The history of humanity is permanently interwoven with doubtful interpretations and bad translations that change the course of events.

As such, sodomy became the *abominable sin*, which literally and etymologically means (in Spanish, *nefando*) the sin that cannot be named. This unspeakable sin will give rise, in the verses of Lord Alfred Douglas, lover of Oscar Wilde, to "The love that dare not speak its name". This is because the real problem of what today we could call the gay question[13] is not literally the sexual, it is not the carnal pleasure *per se*. Throughout human history, people have managed, to have the sex they wanted despite all the prohibitions, mandates, or powers that oppose them. The lists of sexual prohibitions that different cultures brandish to control the pleasures of the body are, at the same time, the enumeration of the pleasures to which humanity surrendered itself, surrenders itself, and will surrender itself. Furthermore, all cultures and power devices are perfectly willing, to a greater or lesser extent, to turn a blind eye to all of this as long as the required discretion is maintained. That is, as long as there is no attempt to alter power relations.

The problem of "homosexuality" never was, nor essentially will be, that of obstacles to the acts, but rather when "homosexuality" seeks to legitimize itself, and, for this, to make itself heard, speaking or writing in the first person.[14] This had already been a problem in classical Greece, where some of Plato's writings are a sustained plea for legitimizing the love between the *erastes and the eromenos*. However, in the cultural orbit of triumphant Christianity, it will take until 1860 for "homosexuality" to begin to speak in the first person.

It occurs for the first time in what was not yet Germany, in the kingdom of Hanover. After being forced to give up his job as a lawyer to avoid a process that could have landed him in jail for his sexual preferences, Karl Heinrich Ulrichs decides not to be ashamed or be silent, he tells his family and friends that he was a *Uranist* (a term that he had coined) and publishes five essays, later compiled in a book entitled *Studies on the Riddle of Male-Male Love*, in which he will give the first modern definition of what, in a very short time, would be called homosexuality: "a female soul trapped in a male body". In this book, Ulrichs creates various neologisms to name the various sexual orientations. Once "homosexuality" and the different ways of living sexuality dare to say their name, they make waves, so to speak, in language, generating modifications and inventions to this day.

It is not possible to be heard without influencing power relations; that is why Ulrichs was also the first activist for the rights of the Uranists, traveling through Germany, always writing and publishing, and always in trouble with the law – due to his statements, not his actions. His books were repeatedly banned and confiscated, which did not, of course, prevent them from being widely circulated anyway. In 1867, he finally managed to speak at the Congress of German Jurists in Munich, where he called for the abolition of the laws against "homosexuality". He managed to speak, but was not able to be heard: he was booed until he had to leave. Regardless, the topic was already established, and it could never be completely ignored again.

At the age of 54, exhausted and feeling that he could no longer do anything else in Germany, he went into exile of his own free will in Italy. In 1895, at the age of 75, he received the only university recognition for his work, an honorary degree from the University of Naples. He died that same year. At the end of his journey, he can have peace in writing:

> Until my dying day, I will look back with pride[15] that I found the courage to come face to face in battle against the specter that, from time immemorial, has been injecting poison into me and into men of my nature. Many have been driven to suicide because all their happiness in life was tainted. Indeed, I am proud that I found the courage to deal the initial blow to the hydra of public contempt.[16]

It is interesting to see what psychiatry does with Ulrichs production. Carl Westphal, a German neurologist and psychiatrist, the inventor of the term *agoraphobia*, gives, in the field of psychiatry, the first modern definition of the "opposite sexual instinct" taking almost literally the definition of Ulrichs: the psyche (instead of the soul) of a woman in the body of a man (and vice versa). I call it the first *modern* definition because it is the first in purely psychological terms – not anatomical, theological, or legal. However, only where Ulrichs called for Uranism to be considered "natural" – that is to say, not pathological, much less criminal – Westphal will make the "contrary sexual instinct" a perversion, a pathology of the assumed sexual instinct.

However, Krafft-Ebing, a psychiatrist who would become very powerful and influential, passing in a very short time from anonymity to fame by publishing his famous *Psychopathia Sexualis* (the main psychiatric reference of the first of Sigmund Freud's famous *Three Essays on the Theory of Sexuality*), confesses in a letter to Ulrichs that "it was only the knowledge of your writings that interested me in such an enormously important field".[17] Yet, he vehemently rejected the idea that homosexuality was somehow "natural", maintained throughout the twelve editions of his book that it was a degenerate and pathological condition, and spoke of Ulrichs and other Uranist writers as frauds "that sought to broaden medical knowledge with foolish gossip about their illnesses".[18]

Freud

If we take *Three Essays on the Theory of Sexuality* as psychoanalysis's foundational text about "sexuality", we will see that it contains both a completely revolutionary approach regarding the way of thinking about sexuality, something never said before, together with a conventional approach, retrograde and normative. This contradiction, in my view (and that of many others), makes psychoanalysis carry a burden of heteronormativity to this day that puts it, in this sense, below its potential. The first of the three essays, of "The Sexual Aberrations", takes an approach that, in a very interesting way, cancels itself out, but neither Freud nor later psychoanalysis, in general, draw the conclusion that follows from that claim: that Freud's development blows up the concept of perversion on which the very text is based. Freud, instead of realizing the consequences of his own approach, remains at the same time with his new theory and with the old (and now outdated) notion of perversion. It is an interesting example of disavowal, a mechanism that psychoanalysis, paradoxically, attributed to the "perversions" themselves.[19]

The notion of perversion on which the entire chapter is based is not a Freudian innovation, but one borrowed without question from nineteenth-century psychiatry, for which perversion was a functional disease of the sexual instinct, defined by its aim, reproduction, and, consequently, by its heterosexual object. Anything sexual outside of that supposedly natural aim would be classified as perverse, from kissing to necrophilia. The continuity that exists apart from the different discursive frameworks between this approach and the secular teaching of the Church about sexuality is evident.

There is a paragraph in Freud's text that surely undoes this idea of the sexual instinct, a paragraph that is so novel and so significant that I am going to quote it verbatim. The paragraph is found at the end of the first section of the book, dedicated solely to "inversion":

> It will be seen that we are not in a position to base a satisfactory explanation of the origin of inversion upon the material at present before us. Nevertheless our investigation has put us in possession of a piece of knowledge which may turn out to be of greater importance to us than the solution of that problem.

Most gay theorists would agree with the first part of the sentence, that of the impossibility of arriving at a satisfactory "explanation" of "inversion", to the point of mistrusting, with very good reason, any attempt to "explain" "homosexuality". Freud continues:

> It has been brought to our notice that we have been in the habit of regarding the connection between the sexual instinct and the sexual object as more intimate than it in fact is. Experience of the cases that are considered abnormal has shown us that in them the sexual instinct and

the sexual object are merely soldered together - a fact which we have been in danger of overlooking in consequence of the uniformity of the normal picture, where the object appears to form part and parcel of the instinct. We are thus warned to loosen the bond that exists in our thoughts between instinct and object. It seems probable that the sexual instinct is in the first instance independent of its object; nor is its origin likely to be due to its object's attractions.

(Freud, 1975 [1905], 12)

Reading this paragraph, we also understand why the book on sexuality opens with the theme of "inversion": "homosexuality" clearly demonstrates the contingency of the object in the field of sexuality. But a few lines further down Freud speaks again of the "Deviations in respect of the sexual aim", and affirms that "The normal sexual aim is regarded as being the union of the genitals in the act known as *copulation*" (15). The text unfolds entirely in the tension between a disintegrated sexuality, which has no natural object, and an evolutionary narrative, present in notions such as fixation, regression, genital primacy, or stages of libido.

Now, the contradiction between these two lines must be specified, and it is only partially apparent. *Since* there is no object for the drive there are cultural devices that regulate sexuality; this could not be otherwise. The problem, as I understand it, is when psychoanalysis re-naturalized these devices in two ways, veiling their historical and contingent character. The first mode of re-naturalization of the *dispositif* of sexuality[20] is that of the libido stages, culminating in the genital stage, mature and, of course, heterosexual. We know to what extent Lacan insisted on pointing out the pitfalls and dangers of this evolutionary path. The second mode is more subtle and not as simple to dismantle: the Oedipus complex.

Lacan

The entire teleological conceptualization of sexuality, with its narrative of the stages of the libido that culminate, in the best of cases, in mature, adult, and, of course, heterosexual genitality, is demolished by the Lacanian critique, which shows what it actually is: ideology with pretensions of science. Lacan teaches us not to think in terms of the individual but the subject, subject of language, and that our life as such takes place on a plane of artificiality, of artifice, without any possibility of returning to any supposedly natural harmony, to no "relation between the sexes".

However, despite all its criticism of the psychoanalytic pastoral, Lacanian theorizing does not escape the regulatory mechanisms of heteronormativity. The articulator of this normative aspect that Lacanian psychoanalysis still preserves is the Oedipus complex, particularly in its articulation with the castration complex.

In general, gay and lesbian studies theorists violently reject all the allegedly phallocentric approaches to psychoanalysis, and I think this is with good reason. How could they not reject an approach that says they are sick and have not reached genital and mature sexuality that places them on the side of perversion or the "unhappy" solutions of the Oedipus complex?[21] In my opinion, they are very right in their rejection, and, at the same time, I agree with the Freudian approach of the phallus as one of the organizers of sexual jouissance. The issue is how to free the theorizing of the phallic phase from the ballast of a heteronormative and, therefore, heterosexist reading.

One complication, in my opinion, is that the Lacanian approach possibly, like the Freudian one on this point, makes the potential for the subject's desire depend too much on the anatomical sexual difference. The "woman" desires a child because she does not have the phallus, which is then homologated to the penis after all, if not, why would it be a "woman" who wants a child?[22] The "woman" looks for the phallus in the "man", who would have it, in turn, for having a penis, and that man, to the extent that he has a penis, could be a father.[23] So, it would seem that subjectivation, access to the desiring dimension and to culture, the possibility of not being totally identified with being the phallus of the Other are all contingent upon the way of positioning oneself in the face of anatomical sexual difference culminating in a heterosexual position and making the phallus coincide with the penis, the vagina with the non-phallus.[24] Moreover, all this is despite the declamation, reiterated over and over again, that the phallus is not the penis.

This is the type of development that leads, logically, to think that a "homosexual" would deny castration, deny difference, because "he would not want to know anything about sexual difference". It leads to the idea, in my opinion very complicated in its clinical consequences, already present in Freud, still current in the discourse of many analysts, that "homosexuals" would be unconsciously attached to a woman (the mother, of course); that each time they transpose "to the masculine object, without interruption, the arousal that she provokes in them"; and that "Their compulsive longing for men has turned out to be determined by their ceaseless flight from women" (Freud, 1975 [1905], 11).

This is a very dangerous idea for two reasons. First, it implicitly contains the notion that "deep down" we all want the same thing, heterosexual intercourse,[25] and that if we don't seek it, it's because we avoid it; we are inhibited by the fear of castration. Second, it is a dangerous idea in the direction of a treatment, because it generates the illusion that then, through analysis, these supposed fears, that "not wanting to know", could be overcome, and, who knows, the patient would finally return to the fold of healthy heterosexuality. The worst thing is that perhaps it may "happen", so enormous is the power of the transference, but, in the long run, as Marguerite Yourcenar already said in 1929, it is a vain struggle.

The matter is very complex because I do not think that psychoanalysis is wrong when it presents the phallus as a major organizer in the field of sexuality, nor would I argue that the phallus has no relation to the materiality of bodies. Just because the phallus *is* not the penis (oh, the verb to be and its dangers!) does not mean that it does not have a privileged relationship with that organ. The organ that represents par excellence the power of the patriarchy, paradoxically, is the weak point of men. The organ that only responds to the power of desire, to what escapes all control. That the phallus plays an important role in the articulation of sexuation, thus, not only puts into play the power of men but also their castration.[26]

The difficulty that psychoanalysis has in escaping from heteronormative *dispositifs* is perhaps due to a fallacy of begging the question in the Oedipal narrative. "Man" and "woman", if we are talking about subjects and not individuals, are signifiers that denote a sexual position that is not solely determined by anatomy, much less by instinct; they are positions that are established at that crossroads of desires, jouissance, prohibitions, longings, fascinations, disappointments, loves, deceptions, which we call the Oedipus complex, and in the complex and heterogeneous social regulations of femininity and masculinity. However, in the classic Oedipal narrative, one speaks of the Oedipus complex "of the girl" and "of the boy", thus putting at the beginning what was supposed to be found at the end: the sexed subjects. At the entrance to the complex, we define them by anatomy, at the exit by desire, and the "happy" ending[27] is considered the one in which the anatomy coincides with what is "normally" expected of that body.

Although in the imaginary anatomy (the anatomy of desire), the phallus can take the form of a penis (and often does), entering Oedipus with a penis does not mean entering as a "man", as a "boy", on the plane of identifications and desire, just as entering without a penis would not prevent leaving with a phallus in the field of desire. This will depend on the very complex interplay between the subject and what they find in the Other's desire, or rather in the field of forces of the crossed desires of the significant Others. This is generally accepted in psychoanalytic theorizing, although it is often conceptualized as deviation or perversion. Where I locate an "epistemological obstacle" of the theory at this point is in the postulation of a necessary heterosexuality in the parents' relationship,[28] which would result in the expected, "happy" heterosexuality of the children.

The experience of homoparental families teaches us that the sexuation of the child depends less on the anatomical sexual differences of the parents than could be deduced from the standard theorization of the Oedipus complex. The children of these families, made up of two dads or two moms, do not show any significant difference in terms of object choice compared to the children of heteropaternal families. That is a very compelling fact that I think we should take note of in order to rethink our categories.

I am going to anticipate criticism: you will say there are later developments of Lacan that allow another reading, mainly those referring to the sexuation formulae. On the one hand, while these developments are very interesting and provide many ideas to think about, they do not contribute much to the perspective that I am taking in this work.[29] In fact, the word "homosexual" practically disappears in Lacan's last seminars and, as far as I know, he never used the word gay. Moreover, he never retracted his repeated claims that homosexuality is a perversion. On the other hand, the sexuation formulae did not prevent Lacan or the Lacanians from being brutally binary and violent with trans-people, as one can clearly see in Lacan's interview with Michel H.,[30] or in the extensive and deplorable Lacanian bibliography on transgenderism.

Yet, the key reason why I stuck mainly to the conceptualization of the Oedipus complex of seminars four and five is that, in my opinion, it is the conceptualization from which the clinic of homosexuality is read in what we could call, paraphrasing Freud, the analytic practice of everyday life. Let us say that, at this point, I am more interested in catechism than in theology because the future of many people depends more on the former than on the latter.

Oedipal prohibition and prohibition of homosexuality

Monique Wittig states in *The Straight Mind* that it is homosexuality, and not incest, which represents the greatest prohibition of "The Straight Mind". I could not say how much of that claim can be sustained,[31] but it led me to some reflections.

All in all, the prohibition of incest restricts, at the most, a few people, with whom almost nobody truly desires to have sexual relations.[32] However, it is true that the structure of kinship would collapse without this prohibition; roles would quickly be confused (the father would be the brother-in-law, the mother the grandmother, and things like that until no one would know what to call themselves, or who they are, or what role they play), and the network of exchanges would gradually disintegrate.

The prohibition of homosexuality is very different: this does prevent many people from living sexuality and love in their own way (well, to be exact, it aims to prevent – prohibiting that which never works). What would be the supposed catastrophe if such a prohibition were lifted? If I put myself in the place of the most homophobic mentalities, I imagine they would say that, if there were only homosexual relationships, it would be the end of humanity; no one would look after the reproduction of the species. Aside from the fact that at this stage of scientific and technological development, which is arguable, the claim itself would be absurd because it would mean that everyone would want to have homosexual relations, which is highly unlikely. Perhaps it is a fantasy that arises from the homosexual desires that underlie the dominant machismo.

However, if the prohibition of homosexuality succeeded (let us assume, for a moment, that fortunately impossible fiction), then a catastrophe would occur: the disappearance of all gay, lesbian, trans, and queer people, and their enormous contribution to culture.

Vanishing points

Not much of the contemporary psychoanalytic literature touches on the issue of homosexuality.[33] I find it, in general, deficient and monotonous, focused on "homosexuality" as a problem, and limited to the central theme Oedipus-phallus-castration, as if *the only* interesting matter was to determine if there is a disavowal of castration, rejection or not of *the* difference, is the only one that seems to count: the anatomical distinction between the sexes. Although I do not say or think that the anatomical sexual difference is insignificant, I do not believe that relevant discourses can be produced on homosexuality, or rather homosexualities, while only considering *that one* difference. Even if we were to grant that the absence of bodies of both sexes in the sex scene and in the fantasies of lesbian and gay people was a sign of a certain "rejection of difference", what then? Is that all there is to say? What relevance would it have in the lives of gay people? What about the contribution of gay people to life and culture? Do gay people only embody a flaw, a disavowal of something that is highly valued in our discourse, which is the anatomical distinction between the sexes. We psychoanalysts, who are, or at least would be expected to be, sensitive to the act of speaking up, to what can be said and what cannot, why do we not read a book like The *Epistemology of the Closet*, by Eve Kosofsky Sedgwick, which makes a brilliant analysis, based on the closet experience, of what the mere fact of being gay determines in terms of enunciation? In my opinion, it is a book from which we will learn significantly more about "homosexuality" than from most psychoanalytic writings.[34] It surprises me that we, psychoanalysts, are not more interested in something that concerns us as much as the phenomenon of the closet and its coming out. Can homosexuality only be thought of negatively in psychoanalytic discourse, for what it is *not*? Do analysts believe that a world without gay people would be better? I do not remember reading a positive assessment of gayness in the psychoanalytic literature (except by Jean Allouch and other members of L'École Lacanienne). Consequently, in mainstream psychoanalysis, I have never come across anything about the devastating effects of homophobia on subjectivity.

§

Someone being gay should be the starting point, not what needs to be explained. Much more important, then, as far as the experience of analysis is concerned, than the question of whether or not the "homosexual" *disavows* castration, seems to me the issue of whether or not it is possible for him to speak up, which in turn is intimately linked to the reception that the subject's word gets, or not. Hence the importance of taking power relations into account because these establish limits to what is said, prohibitions, confession mandates, sanctions, and silences. A child or adolescent who does not respond in their erotic tastes to the expectation of heterosexuality finds themselves subject from the beginning to a particular *discursive regime* (linked, without a doubt, to a *regime of power*), which establishes that something as essential as their eroticism and way of loving must remain outside the discourse, or in the shadows of what is implicit.

If we want to help a subject whose sexuality does not respond to the heterosexual norm, worrying about the *causes* of that sexual choice will not help. This would make sense if the investigation of the supposed causes led to a rectification of the sexual "choice" and if (this is a critical point) that rectification is considered to be desirable, in other words, if it is considered that the ideal would be a world without gay people. It will serve much less to see the causes as a flaw, because under that condition psychoanalysis immediately becomes a normalization device. It is much more interesting, and has a possible transforming effect, to be attentive to the place that this subject has in the discourse that names him and that gives him a place in power relations, that opens or closes possibilities of naming himself, of speaking up to appropriate his body and its jouissance, to establish ties. The gay person, or rather that subject who perhaps calls himself or is called gay (or fag, or dyke, or fruit, or queer, etc.), will know who he is and what his place is as a gay man after the insult. If we do not want to be part of that apparatus, it is a condition that we, analysts, have to review *our* position on. In order to *listen* effectively to a subject who is also gay, I think *The Epistemology of the Closet* is infinitely more useful than the famous *Three Essays*.

§

A gay, a lesbian, has sex with someone not of the other anatomical sex. Are gays more narcissistic, for this reason, than those who seek a partner of the other sex, as some psychoanalytic readings say? Do they look for *themselves* in the sexual encounter? A gay man who desires another man, does he identify with the place of "man"? Does he look for him "as a man"? If someone falls in love with a man, does he necessarily love him as the bearer of the phallus? Does he look for a "man" in the other man? The mere fact of carrying a penis, obviously, does not imply that someone identifies with the place of a man, much less that he identifies himself in all aspects (is there a man who is *completely* a man, except in some fantasies of women, of gays ... and men?). Identifying, what makes us feel included in a certain group, is something very complex, very *composite*, and someone can perfectly identify with the place of man in one aspect and not in another.[35] There is an aspect of identity that is particularly sensitive in terms of eroticism, which is the phallic dimension. Does the subject carry the phallus or is he looking for it? Clearly, the fact that someone was born with a penis does not imply that they identify from the point of view of jouissance with the place of a man as the bearer of the phallus. Within this statement, it is true that there is a mismatch between anatomy and what we could call the anatomy of desire, which is forged in that very subtle play of libidinal forces that we summarize in the notion of the "Oedipus complex". Here the issue, I believe, is to discriminate (but how difficult it is!) if this "mismatch" implies something like *ignorance*, a *rejection* of some reality (that of difference?, that of the lack of a penis in the woman?) or if it is *another way* of positioning oneself concerning the rules of the game: – I already know that I have to get in *that* line,[36] but I like the other one better. Or, maybe – you think *that* line is the one I belong in, but my way of experiencing jouissance, my flesh, tells me that I have to get in the other one.[37] *Another way* that accounts for something different than anatomical reality: the *truth* of the desired field in which the erotic body of that subject was forged. I get the impression that the way in which the Oedipus complex is articulated with the castration complex, based on Freudian theorization, leads us to think that "recognizing", "accepting" "the" difference, or the lack of penis in women, or that only men have a penis, would inevitably lead to a heterosexual choice. Why? Acceptance does not seem to entail any obligation of choice. However, choosing a man (being "a man") or a woman (being "a woman") implies a difference, since I am choosing this and not the other, it is not the same, it is not *undifferentiated*.

Either of the two ways of thinking about this choice, whether as a rejection of reality or as another way of locating oneself, has the drawback of presenting it as if it were voluntary, as if one really *chose* which line to stand in when that seems to be in reality the consequence of the field of libidinal forces to which each subject is exposed. Although, it is quite complex to say what notions such as *acceptance* or *choice* could mean when applied to the times of constitution of the subject. What does a choice mean if it never passed through the consciousness of the subject, never constituted an act, and also (and above all) has no chance of being rectified at a later time?

§

One of the ideas that I want to convey to my colleagues could be expressed as follows: you perhaps believe that a gay person lives in the same world as you (referring, obviously, to analysts who are heterosexual, but with the exception that in the psychoanalytic milieu, except for enormous personal work, even homosexual analysts think "heterosexually"), but you are wrong, a homosexual does not live exactly in the same world as you, just as a poor person does not live in the same world as you, nor a disabled person, nor an immigrant. We are going to have to do a bit of anthropology then, get to know that tribe that lives among us, their relationship customs, their sociability, and the forms of eroticism they practice, which are not the same as those of heterosexuality. The place they occupy in power relations directly determines their place as subjects of discourse (it is not by chance that an expression such as *coming out of the closet*, that is, daring to name something that was silenced-censored, was coined in relation to the gay experience), and the position that you, analysts, take will directly determine what they may or may not say, what they dare not to name, even (especially) in the analysis itself.[38] If you, analysts, do not make an effort to understand that the gay person lives in another world, in a world where the most important thing *is not* whether or not he "disavows" castration (given that, for whatever reason, the fact that their eroticism is directed at their own *anatomical* sex is something that is *not* going to change), but that they can live their life, then I think that you are going to be of very little help to that subject who in the first instance, and for whatever reasons, trusted you.

§

The question that has generally guided the theoretical developments of psychoanalysis regarding homosexuality has been: how did homosexuality originate, and not, what can we learn, clinically and theoretically, from LGBTQI + people? How can we help them? My goal is to change the perspective and shift the focus from the supposed interest of the theory onto that of the LGBTQI + analysand. The real problem of gay people, in terms of being gay, homophobia, far exceeds what is possible to solve in the analyst's office. Although, if the analyst positions themselves well toward these issues (that is, if they reorient their listening regarding how to deal with homosexuality) they can be a huge support by helping the analysand deal with homophobia with more resources, meanwhile, assisting them in overcoming their inhibitions, symptoms, and anxieties.

Notes

1 I refer to the psychoanalysis of the most powerful institutions as "hegemonic". These institutions are also the ones that monopolize the transmission in the universities (at least in Argentina, where psychoanalysis has a strong presence in the universities).

2 "Homosexual", gay, or faggot? Elucidating this matter of vocabulary would require a separate writing since they by no means have the same semantic resonances. Let us just say that the first denomination was seized by psychiatry from a pamphlet written in defense of the rights of those who were, until that moment, Sodomites, Uranists, or Inverts. The second prevails after the events of Stonewall in 1969, or, in other words, the birth of a gay liberation movement. "Faggot" would be the most common and traditional vernacular of calling the one who, with the liberation movement, would become gay. In the first instance, it has an insulting character, although it was re-appropriated as a "decontextualized citation of the insult" (Butler). Personally, I feel it to be too aggressive, except in the use between gay people, that is, between faggots.

3 It is true that "homosexual" or "gay" are not psychoanalytic categories. However, neither are "man" or "woman", "boy" or "girl", yet we use them profusely without further questioning.

4 Some colleagues tell me things like: "I don't care who my patient has sex with. It does not matter to me if they're straight or gay". It may be a non-judgmental attitude, which I value, but this whole book tries to convey that the most important thing is not if it does not matter to the analyst, but that it *does matter*

to the analysand; they are not indifferent to being gay or not. If not for this, we establish a false symmetry between hetero and homosexuality.

5 Miquel Bassols, a psychoanalyst from the AMP, in a book in which he responds to the intervention from Paul B. Preciado before the École de la Cause Freudienne, affirms that Preciado "vindicates a« trans »condition, a way of being that *feels* caged by the dominant discourses on sexuality and its genders" (Miquel Bassols, 2021, 10. Italics are mine).

6 Reading Foucault changed my idea of what *the Other* is; it made me think about the Other in a way that is more complex, more open, considering more varied and more complex *dispositifs* for producing subjectivity. As I said above, when I think of the Other, I do not limit myself either to language (the treasure of the signifier) or to the parents, or the mother (the oedipal).

7 On several occasions, I will warn against a certain use of the "case-by-case basis" argument, typically utilized to discredit any generalization, and thereby depoliticize theory. I hope that in the context it is clear why I do it: not because it does not seem fundamental to me, but because, if we only put the accent there, we run the risk of believing that we are dealing with individuals who found themselves in their singularity (omitting all the determinations of race, class, gender, nationality, sexuality, etc.), and then, wanting to rescue the singularity as much as possible, we naively fall into all the delusions of the ego. The singularity is always in a dialectical relationship with the generality; I try to remember this because it has important consequences in the direction of the treatment.

8 Throughout this book, I am going to refer many times to "power relations". It is a concept of Michel Foucault that I adopted because I find it very enabling. As his work progresses, Foucault becomes increasingly concerned with power, how it is exercised, how it is represented, and how it changes in the way it is exercised. He argues that the West theorized power in a juridical-discursive way. It is the power thought of in terms of law, which about sex can only say no: prohibition, censorship, punishment. His mode of operation is Law and speech. It is how psychoanalysis, in general, has thought of power. To this way of representing power, Foucault opposes his model, based on the idea of multiple power relations, power mechanisms that function not on the basis of right, but on technique; not on the basis of law, but on normalization; not on the basis of punishment, but on control. These mechanisms are exercised in levels and forms that go beyond the State and its apparatuses. In Foucault's theory, power is not something that one has or lacks; no one is outside of power relations, and no one ceases to exercise a certain form of power. That is why they are called power *relations* because power is never someone's attribute but rather a strategic relationship of forces. It is a much more dynamic way of thinking about the question of power, and that, by moving away from the idea of a single focus of Power, allows us to think (said in Lacanian jargon) that the Other is never omnipotent.

9 "Relations of power are not in a position of exteriority with respect to other types of relationships (economic processes, knowledge relationships, sexual relations), but are immanent in the latter; they are the immediate effects of the divisions, inequalities, and dis-equilibriums which occur in the latter, and conversely they are the internal conditions of these differentiations; relations of power are not in superstructural positions, with merely a role of prohibition or accompaniment; they have a directly productive role, wherever they come into play". (Foucault, 1978, 94).

10 When speaking of the "Other of the time", in the singular, power relations are unknown, assuming an Other equal for all.

11 Cited from Beatriz Preciado, *Terrorismo anal.*

12 I thank Mark Jordan, author of a wonderful book called *The Invention of Sodomy in Christian Theology*, for clarifying this point for me with his usual kindness.

13 It is the denomination that Didier Eribon chooses in another excellent book, which is precisely called, *in French, Réflexions sur la question gay, and that was translated into English as Insult and the Making of the Gay Self.*

14 Let us remember Proust's famous advice to Gide: "You can tell everything, but on condition that you never say I".

15 Here the word "pride" already appears, something which will acquire so much importance in the struggles of gays and lesbians as a political response to the induction of shame.

16 Condensed in this paragraph, we find the two elements of what I called the gay experience: insult and the experience of the closet, along with a powerful response to both. Added 2022: I sometimes wondered why I included these words from Ulrichs in this book. I wondered if they were relevant to the subject of the book. However, I never decided to cut them. Checking the text for its English translation, I seemed to understand what I was trying to say and whom I was addressing. It is not just about making history; it is a message, addressed to my colleagues, that aims to point out a direction, even a direction for a treatment. "You see, the important thing for this 'homosexual', as you like to call him, was having taken the floor and having influenced power relations. That *act*, which required strength and courage, is what allows him to be proud until the day he dies. It is a bid for life and against death". Moreover, it is not a metaphor, as Ulrichs reminds us when evoking those who were driven to suicide by the poison of homophobia, and suicide is only the exacerbated and tragic expression of so many lives deprived of enjoyment, of so many deaths in life. Knowing whether or not "the homosexual" denies castration is of negligible importance with respect to what is at stake in that act. Colleagues, let's not think small. Some time ago, I was asked what the publication of *this book* had meant to me. "I can die in peace", I said without hesitation.

17 Quoted in Francis Mark Mondimore, *A natural history of homosexuality.*

18 Idem.

19 All of this development is based on the extraordinary book by Arnold Davidson, *The Emergence of Sexuality*, which I cannot recommend enough.

20 Deployment of sexuality, or *dispositif* of sexuality (Michel Foucault) is a concept that accounts for the relations of power with sex. Coming from a psychoanalytic background, the idea of the "heterogeneity of the deployment" opened up my way of thinking about sexuality: there is no single, global, valid strategy for the whole society in the relations of power with sexuality. The Oedipus complex is just one more element of a much more complex and comprehensive apparatus. The deployment of sexuality is thought of in opposition to the deployment of alliance (the one that traditionally governed sexual relations in all societies – marriage, kinship, heritage); in general terms, this deployment of alliance is the one that is taken into account in psychoanalytic theory. The *dispositif* of sexuality is typical of modernity, and it is what creates sexuality as a specific field. This multiple deployment is at the origin and is the effect of the proliferation of discourses on sexuality that has occurred since the eighteenth century. It is made up, for Foucault, of four major strategic groups: the hysteria of the female body, the pedagogization of the child's sex, the socialization of procreative behaviors, and the one that most interests us in this book – the psychiatrization of perverse pleasure. I use this concept somewhat in my own way, which will become clear as it is read, above all, to emphasize that there are many other devices, in addition to the Oedipal, to regulate sexualities.

21 "If, therefore, little Hans reaches a *happy solution* to the crisis he has entered, it is surely worthwhile asking ourselves whether at the end of this crisis we may deem this to be a completely normal dissolution of the Oedipus complex". (Lacan, 2020, 314).

> ...it's only through the intermediary of a certain position adopted in relation to the phallus - for the woman, as lack, for the man, as threatened – that what presents itself as what will be, let's say, the *best outcome* [l'issue, disons, la plus heureuse] necessarily comes about.
>
>   (Lacan, 2017, 309) (Emphasis mine)

22 I think of all the efforts and sacrifices that a gay patient made to be able to have a child, and it becomes clear to me that the desire for a child does not have a necessary relationship with the lack of a penis.

23 "...there is someone [the father] who can respond come what may, and who in every case answers that he is the one who's got the true phallus, *the real penis*. He is the one who holds the trump card, and who knows it". (Lacan, 2020, 201) (Emphasis mine).

24 We know, however, that the following two facts depend on it [the castration complex] - that on one side the boy becomes a man, that on the other side the girl becomes a woman. (Lacan, 2017, 170).

25 Something which may be true (it would be called top-bottom in gay eroticism and butch-femme in lesbian), but not in the genital sense.

26 That is something that we could respond to the theorists who criticize psychoanalysis because it would be phallocentric. Although, of course, if we want to make ourselves heard, it would be good for us to listen too.

27 See note 21.

28 The matter is very complex; perhaps there will always be heterosexuality on the phallic level, but not necessarily on the genital level.

29 After the publication of the first edition of the book, I understood that there is a more important reason for having omitted a development based on Lacan's famous (perhaps too famous) sexuation formulae. The central theme of my book is not homosexuality, nor gayness, but rather heteronormativity, homophobia, the deployment of sexuality, and how they affect the production of subjectivities, their stigmatization (with the concomitant suffering they produce), and the discourse and practice of psychoanalysis. The sexuation formulae, as far as I understand them, try to account for sexuation (always thought in a binary way) from two modes of jouissance. Inferences could be made regarding homophobia based on these considerations (the rejection of feminine jouissance, for example), but I prefer to address the issue from other discourses that deal specifically with what interests me.

30 Lacan, J., «Entretien avec Michel H.», en Frignet H. *Sur l'identité sexuelle: à propos du transsexualisme*. Paris: Editions de l'Association freudienne; 1996, p. 312.

31 However, it is certain that the structuralist theorization of the prohibition of incest implicitly excludes any relationship that is not heterosexual.

32 I do not delve here into the complex issue of domestic sexual abuse.

33 There is an abundant bibliography on the subject in the field of what Lacanians call post-Freudians. In general terms, it is much more heteronormative than the texts of Freud or Lacan. Those who resisted the removal of homosexuality from the DSM the most were not psychiatrists, but psychoanalysts.

34 Just as "Las malas", by Camila Sosa Villada, teaches us much more about trans people than any psychoanalytic text I know.

35 An analysand told me: "I am a man, until I take off my briefs".

36 The mechanisms of heteronormativity will remind him over and over again, with violence if necessary, that *he belongs* in that line. But, gosh, desire is so stubborn!

37 This of course opens up the interesting question of whether there are two lines or more.

38 On some occasions I have received gay patients in second analyses who reported interventions in their previous analyses that denoted sometimes very subtle ways of censoring their gayness, that delayed or prevented them for a long time from assuming their way of living eroticism and love, and that also harmed the exercise of the *fundamental rule* of analysis.

Bibliography

Bassols, M. (2021). *La diferencia de los sexos no existe en el inconsciente. Sobre un informe de Paul B. Preciado dirigido a los psicoanalistas.* Buenos Aires: Grama.

Davidson, A. (2004). *The emergence of sexuality.* Cambridge, MA and London: Harvard University Press.

Eribon, D. (2004). *Insult and the making of the gay self.* Durham, NC and London: Duke University Press.

Foucault, M. (1978). *The history of sexuality, Volume 1: An introduction.* New York, NY: Pantheon Books.

Freud, S. (1975 [1905]). *Three essays on the theory of sexuality.* New York, NY: Basic Books.

Jordan, M. (1997). *The invention of sodomy in Christian theology.* Chicago, IL and London: The University of Chicago Press.

Kosofsky Sedgwick, E. (1990). *Epistemology of the closet.* Berkeley; Los Angeles and London: University of California Press.

Lacan, J. (2017). *The formations of the unconscious. The seminar of Jacques Lacan, Book V.* Cambridge: Polity Press.

Lacan, J. (2019). *Desire and its interpretation. The seminar of Jacques Lacan Book VI.* Cambridge: Polity Press.

Lacan, J. (2020). *The object relation. The seminar of Jacques Lacan, Book IV.* Cambridge: Polity Press.

Wittenberger, G. and Christfried, T. (Eds.). (2002). *Las circulaers del "Comité Secreto" 1921* [The circular letters of the "Secret Committee" 1921]. Madrid: Editorial Síntesis.

Wittig, M. (1992). *The straight mind.* Boston, MA: Beacon Press.

2 The original entanglement. How psychoanalysis could not escape the heteronorm

Sexuality, like the symptom, is disruptive. It never quite fits. As Freud says in the *Introductory Lectures on Psychoanalysis*, only half in jest, it is the unseemly, which should not be talked about. It also happens to be something that we do not stop talking about. The relationship between symptom and sexuality is the cornerstone of psychoanalysis, the affirmation of a *necessary* relationship between the two. Freud defended it with courage and stubbornness.

However, the reading that he made of this relationship between the symptom and sexuality could not escape something that was far removed from his conceptual scheme: what Foucault called the *deployment of sexuality* or *dispositif of sexuality*, and which I, basing myself on other authors, would prefer to call the *dispositif of heterosexuality, or heteronormativity, or compulsory heterosexuality*. What Foucault taught me (and what radically changed my way of thinking) is the political dimension of sexuality. I thought of sexuality in terms of desire, jouissance, intimacy, fantasy, or the *psychic* conflict that is inevitably associated with sexuality, which I believe happens to most psychoanalysts. The only point, important by the way, where sexuality was linked with politics (but I did not think of it in those terms) was when it included the dimension of prohibition, generally reduced to the prohibition of incest. Foucault taught me how much more vast, complex and essential the political dimension of sexuality is and that the prohibitive aspect of the regulation of sexualities is always linked to a prescriptive aspect. Sexuality cannot be thought of without taking politics into account.[1] Sure, Foucault was gay, which immediately made him much more sensitive because he suffered from this heteronormative political dimension of sexuality.

Let us begin with a definition of "heteronormativity". I take the one from Wikipedia in Spanish, because it seems very clear and precise: "*Heteronorm or heteronormativity*" is a social, political and economic regime that imposes heterosexual practices through various mechanisms which include (artistic, educational, religious, legal, etc.); and through various institutions that present heterosexuality as necessary for the functioning of society and

DOI: 10.4324/9781003252160-3

as the only valid model of sex-affective relationship and kinship. The regime reinforces itself with social mechanisms such as marginalization, invisibility, or persecution.

> It is based on a dichotomous and hierarchical system. This includes the idea that all human beings are divided into two distinct and complementary categories: male and female; that sexual and marital relations are normal only between people of different sexes; and that each sex has certain natural roles in life. Thus, physical sex, gender identity and the social role of gender should frame any person within entirely masculine or feminine norms. Consequently, heterosexuality is considered the only normal sexual orientation. The norms that this term describes or criticizes may be overt, covert, or implied. Those who identify and criticize heteronormativity say that it warps discourse by stigmatizing different concepts of both sexuality and gender and making certain types of self-expression more difficult.
>
> ("Heteronormatividad", 2022, para. 2)[2]

This is what Freud did not manage to measure in its full magnitude, that political dimension of sexuality. It is not that he was completely unaware of it (there are Freud's eminently social texts to prove it), but his conceptual framework, his historical moment, and his own singularity (apparently he was heterosexual[3]) did not allow him to conceptualize all the complexity of what Foucault defined as "power relations". Freud tends to speak of *the* culture as if it were a stable and homogeneous thing, not subject to constant struggle, and regarding sexuality, as if its role was eminently prohibitive. He thinks about the regulation of sexuality within the framework of the family and the Oedipal. Although, it is enough for someone not to accommodate compulsory heterosexuality for them to collide with a regulatory apparatus that goes far beyond the family environment. I am going to take an example to illustrate what I am referring to with this term of power relations, and how they can operate to keep the *dispositif* of compulsory heterosexuality functioning. This is a message sent by a friend, Emiliano Blanco (who authorized me to use it for this book), to some of his contacts, deeply affected after having experienced a situation of homophobic violence. His anxiety and courage will help us to see how the heteronorm operates in the neighborhood, far from the family and the State:

> *I come to beg for empowerment. Today, Sunday, I met a young person who I'm getting to know little by little. After a delicious brunch, we went out to the street to celebrate our gay meeting and we talked and laughed … without thinking, we walked hand in hand. Then we had an encounter with the criterion of legitimizing reality. On a sidewalk near Plaza de Mayo[4] there were three young men drinking beer and listening to pop from the 1980s. We*

thought that it came from some bar and despite our surprise that it was their music, we continued advancing ... to which I was struck with a stone (which did nothing but collide with my back...) accompanied by a scream: FAG-GOTS, DON'T WALK ON OUR STREETS ... FAGGOTS!!! YOUSH-OULD BE KILLED ... FAGGOTS!!! I stopped, my hookup too ... we looked at each other and I thought to continue, while my hookup asked me if I was okay. I grabbed the stone, and advanced towards them. The police were on the corner seeing everything. I approach and tell the guy: this is yours, it does not belong to me. The tough guy looks at me defiantly and tells me: YOU'RE A FUCKING FAGGOT, YOU'RE DISGUSTING. He spits in my face ... I didn't think about it for a second ... I gave a tremen-dous KICK to his stereo that bounced off his stomach. And I yelled at him: YOU'RE A FAGGOT KILLER!!! AND YOU ARE THE ONES WHO ARE GOING TO HAVE TO KILL YOUR HATE!!! The police arrive, they separate us ... because they were going to comejump me. The police saw everything and I told the officer: You saw that they threw the stone at me ... and he replied: THEY ARE DRUNK. I retorted: THEY STILL WANT TO KILL US!!! Then the tough guy comes and throws a punch at me (but this dancer[5] has very good reflexes), I dodge him and punch him hard in the face ... he was bleeding a lot and I got scared. But I couldn't help but rejoice in that situation and tell him: YOU SEE HOW IT'SNOT THE FAGGOT'S BLOOD THAT'S DRIPPING ... STUPID!!! The po-lice suggested that I go ... that we go. And I did ... without fear. I kissed my hookup ... and we continued walking with a euphoria that continues to electrify the hand that I hit him with. I never threw a punch ... I was always afraid of a situation like this. I feel kind of confused ... but with a certain peace at the same time. Well ... I needed to share it, because I'm sick of these things happening to us!!!

Let us suppose that an analysand tells us of a similar situation (there are many like this). The error which we can commit as psychoanalysts (an error with serious consequences for many people) would be to read this "encoun-ter with the criterion of legitimizing reality" in purely *psychological* terms, in terms of the subjectivities at stake, as if it were individuals who act outside of a sexual regimen. It is essential when reading this scene not to lose sight of the apparatus that authorizes these young men to shout FAGGOTS, to make death threats. It is something that goes far beyond its singularity, it could have been others, and still, it would have been exactly the same. The important thing is to understand that there is a sexual order, that which we call heteronormativity, which justifies that scream and encourages it to be uttered, and which makes it, in addition to an insult, a *quote*. It has already been shouted countless times, and it will be uttered again if this sexual order prevails. It does not take courage to do it. This scene recounted by Emiliano shows that there is an order that authorizes, or rather prescribes, marginali-zation and inferiority to any form of sexuality that does not respond to the heterosexual norm. This determines that public space is a heterosexual one ("don't walk on *our* sidewalks"). The little chronicle is much more instructive because it shows how a subject *can give a response* that alters power relations, both in that beautiful and civilized gesture of returning the stone (in that brave act, performatively, institutes the stone as something that "does not belong to him"), as in the kick or punch, the appeal to the police who observe everything but who justifies ("they are drunk"), and, of course, when saying that it is them, the homophobic tough guys, who are going to have to kill their hatred. The most beautiful thing is the response the final kiss. There is a resistance to the heteronormative order in the message that he shared with those of us who were going to understand and accompany him.[6] The punch line of the message reminds us how a subject who does not respond to the heterosexual norm is *permanently* put through this kind of violence: "I needed to share it, because I'm sick of these things happening to us!!!"

Foucault posits that no one has *the* power, and no one is completely powerless, which is why he speaks in terms of "power relations". "Power is everywhere; not because it embraces everything, but because it comes from everywhere" (Foucault, 1978, 93). Power relations allow Emiliano to exercise resistance to the heteronormative power that is embodied in the young men who drank beer and listened to eighties pop. While it does not take courage to launch a homophobic attack, it does take courage to respond. It is important not to lose sight of the fact that if Emiliano can give that answer, it is because he is not alone. Otherwise, there is a risk of reducing it to a *subjective* response (which, of course, it is as well), in the sense of an *individual* response, losing sight of the fact that it is because of a prolonged, huge *collective* struggle that he may not submit to the "criterion of legitimating reality". In another historical moment, not far away, not only would that response have been literally unimaginable, but it would also not have been possible for two young men to walk hand in hand down the street (the public space was not in dispute, *it was* effectively only heterosexual). Another gay kid could have kept quiet, continued on his way as if nothing had happened, or not have dared to walk hand in hand with his couple, there is without a doubt a singular dimension to the answer, but one that is linked to a historical dimension embedded in power relations that produce different subjectivities in different contexts (historical, cultural, class, gender, etc.), which establish the field of the possible-permitted and the impossible-prohibited, of the representable-thinkable and the unrepresentable-unthinkable, and that even marks limits to the possibility of transgressing.

How does psychoanalysis position itself with respect to this political dimension of sexuality? In my opinion, in general terms, badly. Despite the fact that in many ways psychoanalytic theory constituted an important step in the struggle that has been taking place in the western world to rethink the relationships of genders and sexualities. Psychoanalysis, sometimes in a clear and evident way, other times in much more subtle ways (but perhaps for that very reason more dangerous) remained too taken up by this *dispositif* of heterosexuality, and then, going against its own spirit remains at this point on the side of the normalizing devices and not on that of those that enable the diversity (although, curiously, this is often done in the name of *the* difference).

When Freud begins his own investigation, detaching himself from the hypnotic method and following the clues that Breuer had noticed, he finds that behind the symptom there is something sexual, which he first interprets as traumas, then as desires and fantasies. This is how he concludes on a *sexual* etiology of the neuroses. Although Freud could not (he could not do all the work himself!) question the concepts, which were not simple at all, he used to think of that thing called "sexuality". If we look at this from Foucault's perspective, it is Freud's blind spot. It is reflected in what I call the *original entanglement*, which, like any point of origin, is arbitrary and mythical. I locate the *original entanglement* in the famous statement in *Three Essays on the Theory of Sexuality* that "neuroses are, so to say, the negative of perversions" (Freud, 1975 [1905], 31). In that statement, I identify the point at which psychoanalysis begins to be uncritically trapped in the *dispositif* of heterosexuality.

Let us start with the notion of *perversion* that sustains the text of *Three Essays*, which is none other than the one posited by psychiatry of his time.[7] Any sexuality that is not heterosexual-genital-reproductive is perverse. To such an extent that the kiss, according to Freud's statement, would be perverse, strictly speaking, and only convention makes us not consider it that way. And that the divide between what is considered *neurosis* and *perversion* would be determined by modes of sexuality (by object and aim) shows the intervention of the dispositif of sexuality (a social, political, and economic regime, historically situated) determining the theorization of subjectivity.[8] What a coincidence that the line of demarcation that separates one field from the other goes through what the heteronormative regime prescribes! I understand that neurosis is a conflict in the subject who defends themself against certain forms of jouissance that are their own[9] but that collide with their narcissistic identifications and with the ideals that support them. Having made the theorization of this conflict depend on the way that adopts sexuality was a first step to placing psychoanalysis on the side of normalization devices. Against its own essence.

The most paradoxical thing is that in this same text Freud posits a powerful conceptual tool to dismantle the heteronormative regime, which is authentically psychoanalytic, and breaks with psychiatric thought. This is the most important statement, by far, in the entire text. We quote it again: "It has been brought to our notice that we have been in the habit of regarding the connection between the sexual instinct and the sexual object as more intimate than it in fact is" (Freud, 1975 [1905], 12). With this statement Freud loses the support of the psychiatric conception of perversion (which was none other than the existence of a sexual instinct to which an object and an aim were inherent), but, to the detriment of many people, he does not become aware of the ultimate consequences of his statement. If the object of the drive is, as Freud states, contingent, then "perversion" as it is defined in the text, is no longer supported: an instinct that does not exist cannot be perverted.[10]

In his first important text on *other sexualities*, Freud introduces the Trojan horse of the psychiatric conception of sexuality into psychoanalytic theory, which is nothing more than one more element of a control and surveillance *dispositif* for sexualities. The text does not start with listening to the subjects, but with the psychiatric classification and, by not relying on its own postulate to read it critically, arrives at the erroneous conclusion that neurosis has a direct relationship with how sexuality is experienced (very different from saying that it has a direct relationship with eroticism). It expulses, then, everyone who is not "heterosexual" into the field of the perverse (of the "extremely bad, that intentionally causes harm" or "that corrupts the customs or the usual order and state of things", according to the Royal Spanish Academy), where they are not listened to in his subjective conflict, but rather classified according to his way of experiencing sexuality. Consequently, the text *naturalizes and ratifies* the *dispositif* of sexuality by making the psychiatric regulation of sexuality the line of demarcation of different subjectivities.

With the Oedipus complex in its articulation with the castration complex, a much more decisive step is taken to leave psychoanalysis on the side of the mechanisms that try to normalize sexual diversity. As it is articulated in psychoanalytic doxa, it is an artifice to produce heterosexuality. Perhaps the problem is not that the Oedipus complex produces heterosexuality, but that it imposes it. Since the drive lacks a naturally adequate object, it is logical that the *infans* subject is offered one and identifying models to face an erotic life. It does not seem too far-fetched to me that "girls" are offered "feminine"[11] identifications and ideals, and the "boys" are offered "masculine". It is too much to ask each subject to invent from scratch a stylization of erotic life. No, I do not think that is where the problem lies, but in what response we give and how we theorize when the *infans* subject does not respond as expected to the models and ideals that are offered. Violence begins when we go from proposing a style of gender and sexuality to wanting to impose it based on anatomy, and when we believe that there are only two possible and "natural" styles of erotic life.

To give an example of this persistent difficulty of psychoanalysis to think about other sexualities, I am going to make a brief comment on a paragraph from the book *Lágrimas de lo real*,[12] by Norberto Rabinovich.[13] In Chapter XII, *El goce de la perversión*,[14] this 2007 book continues to locate perversion in terms of sexual behavior, exactly as Krafft-Ebing did, since it states that "the outstanding point that allows us to more rigorously identify the perverse lies in the avoidance of heterosexual genital coupling" (Rabinovich, 2007, 139). Therefore, and as the author explicitly acknowledges, homosexuality, as well as all non-heterosexual sexuality, would necessarily be on the side of perversion, which is in tune with Lacan's conception, who always referred to homosexuality (when he referred to it) as a perversion. From this statement, it will be impossible to think of other sexualities as what they truly are, they will always be read in terms of what they are not, of hetero-sexuality. A homosexual choice would be, for example, a non-heterosexual choice, an *avoidance* of the heterosexual choice. Since this is not, after all, a text from 1905, this is going to be linked to the castration complex. "Sexual perversions would arise as a result of a marked disavowal of castration, which arouses in them a fear, at least a little greater than in neurotics" (Rabinovich, 2007, 139). "They" are all those who do not enjoy sex while in the canonical form, the one that responds to the heteronorm. We must recognize that the author admits that, as an index of differentiation with respect to neurosis, this one, based on sexual behaviors, is a bit weak in the matter of degrees, of something "a little bigger" (Rabinovich, 2077, 139).[15]

With this, the necessary conditions for a naturalization of heterosexual-ity are already given, no matter how much it is denied in the discourse. If it seems that I am exaggerating, I offer a sentence as a sample and demon-stration from the same text: "We can then conjecture that the pervert fears going to the *predestined place* of sexual coupling" (Rabinovich, 2007, 141).[16] Once there is a *predestined place*, the contingency of the object is lost and we reintroduce God into the equation. With this, I do not want to deny the rel-evance of the castration complex, there is much clinically verifiable in what psychoanalysis posits in this regard. My proposal is to find ways of thinking about it that take psychoanalysis out of the heteronormative trap in which it is placed and (much worse) in which it places its analysands if it does not review the articulation of these concepts.

Notes

1 Nor can it be thought of without a reference to love, desire, and jouissance. That is where psychoanalysis made unavoidable contributions.
2 https://es.wikipedia.org/wiki/Heteronormatividad.
3 I say "apparently" because there are two enigmatic points in Freud's sexual life. One is that his only love affair, apparently, was with a woman named Martha, with whom his sex life was very poor; the other is how paranoid he got when Marie Bonaparte bought the correspondence from Fließ, because, according to him, the letters revealed a "homosexual" bond.
4 Plaza de Mayo (May Square) is a city square and the main foundational site of Buenos Aires, Argentina.
5 Emiliano is a very good dancer.
6 In fact, by including it in this book, I retransmit it and amplify its reach.
7 In fact, the main psychiatrists who forged that notion of sexuality and its pathol-ogy, that is, perversion, are cited by Freud as a reference on the first page of the text.
8 I am not positing that a subject could be thought of outside of power relations. The problem is different: that these power relations are to be naturalized and equated, for example, with "culture", in universal terms, or with "nature".

9 Jouissance that is their "own" in a very particular way, because being very much their own, is also something completely foreign, that in which, in the first instance, the subject does not recognize their self. Freud called it drive.

10 Regarding this point, I recommend the excellent text by Arnold I. Davidson, The emergence of sexuality, Harvard University Press, 2004.

11 Related, but different, is the issue of how each era's culture, social class, etc. defines what is feminine and what is masculine.

12 *Tears of the Real.*

13 Norberto Rabinovich is a renowned Argentine analyst.

14 *Jouissance of the Perversion.*

15 Something that, with the same honesty, he reaffirms in the last sentence of this paragraph: "in any case, there is not a detail in this description that cannot be transferred to the level of neuroses. The difference is, in principle, a matter of accents" (Rabinovich, 2007, 142).

16 The italics are mine.

Bibliography

Davidson, A. (2004). *The emergence of sexuality.* Cambridge, MA and London: Harvard University Press.

Foucault, M. (1978). *The history of sexuality, Volume 1: An introduction.* New York, NY: Pantheon Books.

Freud, S. (1975 [1905]). *Three essays on the theory of sexuality.* New York, NY: Basic Books.

Freud, S. (1963). *The standard edition of the complete psychological works of Sigmund Freud, Volume XVI (1916–1917).* London: The Hogarth Press.

Rabinovich, N. (2007). *Lágrimas de lo real.* Rosario: Homo Sapiens Ediciones.

3 Oedipus reloaded

Transcription of the conference presented in Santiago de Chile, within the framework of the Monthly Meetings of Lacantera Freudiana,[1] on October 21, 2017.

According to my research for this presentation, in Chile, President Michelle Bachelet presented a marriage equality bill. A little late considering her electoral promises, and forced by the Inter-American Court of Human Rights, but on August 31, she presented it. If the project is approved in Congress, Chile would join the 23 countries so far (out of a total of 193 or 195 countries – there is no agreement!) that have so-called equal marriage.[2] Here the word "equal" appears, which already brings us to the issue of equality, and, therefore, given the oppositional structure of the signifier, of difference.[3]

Same-sex marriage is a topic that generates controversy wherever it is discussed. This is logical since, concerning this project, two outlooks of life continue to confront each other, the religious versus the secular, or that of the sign versus the signifier, and the guaranteed order versus that of invention. It has a complex relationship with the opposition in social sciences of essentialist versus constructivist positions. We could locate the origin of this confrontation (somewhat mythically, as happens with any origin narrative) in the very complex confrontation of powers that erupted with the French Revolution, and its famous maxim of *freedom, equality, fraternity.* There we have equality again, which returns in the concept of marriage-equality. The secular project is that of modernity, and it is new; the religious vision is that of tradition.

Two years after The Declaration of the Rights of Man and the Citizen, the writer and political philosopher Olympe de Gouges (1748–1793) drafted the text of the Declaration of the Rights of Woman and the Citizen. The "equality" of the Declaration of the Rights of Man and the Citizen was exactly what its title indicates, equality between men, males. Although, once this first fall of the monarchy as a regime and of divine right takes place, the place of women is no longer delimited by what tradition sacralized, and a rethinking of the relations between the genders begins that lasts until

DOI: 10.4324/9781003252160-4

today. The latest expression of this struggle (because it is a struggle, like everything that questions existing power relations) in my country is the *Ni una menos*[4] movement, which seeks to put an end to the very serious problem of femicide. It is within the framework of destabilization of relations between genders that progress in the struggle of *other* sexualities becomes possible. For these other sexualities to be able to speak up and claim their rights, the patriarchal order had to be weakened, and that began with the questioning of the place of women, by women (this is very important, no one handed them their rights, just as no one is going to hand them to the lesbians, gays, or trans people).

Let us get back to the topic of same-sex marriage. What do its critics say? Informing myself about the situation in Chile, I found Father Patricio's website (padrepatricio.com) that gives 18 reasons to oppose homosexual "marriage" (thus, in quotes), which he considers an "anthropological lie" and "legal nonsense". Although it gives 18 reasons, the first and main one, as the page consistently states, says that same-sex marriage "implies distorting the concept of marriage."

> The most important reason - from which the others derive - is that with the Government's law, the concept of marriage will change. It will no longer be, as in recent millennia, the union of a man and a woman, but also that of two men or two women. Which implies perverting the nature of things.

When speaking of "perverting the nature of things", Father Patrick assumes that there is a natural order of things (such as marriage) and that any other way of understanding it is to deviate from that natural order. However, we find here another word that has a long and, in my opinion, not a very honorable history: "to pervert". It is the incidence of evil, although against the background of a "natural" order that is indistinguishable from the "sacred" order. The word will make history first in psychiatry, and then, alas, in psychoanalysis.

However, the secular version says that the meaning of marriage is subject to changes in history and social usage, and that its meaning can change so much as to lead to a modification in the law. It says, therefore, that no father can say, once and for all, what is the nature of men, women, and their adequate relationships.

Clearly psychoanalysis is unthinkable in the religious worldview of Father Patrick. Precisely one of Lacan's most important teachings was to draw our attention to the structure of the signifier, and to the impossibility of fixing a meaning, while establishing a univocal relationship between a word and its meaning, which is what Father Patricio wants. One might think, then, that psychoanalysts would be inclined to be in favor of same-sex marriage, or at least not against it. However, things are more complex than that. This was clearly seen in France, where there was a strong discussion of this law in which psychoanalysts also intervened. Although many clarified that there was nothing in psychoanalytic theory that would allow marriage equality to be opposed on its behalf, it was necessary because there were others who argued, on behalf of Lacanian-oriented psychoanalytic theory, that marriage equality would be a catastrophe, basing this assertion on the conceptualization of the Oedipus complex. This disparity of opinions reflects, in my opinion, the contradictions that exist in the various psychoanalytic theories regarding this issue.[5] Precisely regarding the issue that was, at the origin of psychoanalysis, its stumbling stone, sexuality, the theory oscillates between the two versions, the one I called the secular and the other religious.

Reading myself

Having to prepare this presentation (my first one that was not in Argentina) and taking advantage of the fact that I have written several articles, I took the opportunity to read myself. I would almost say that to read Jorge Reitter, after having written the texts for a while they, fortunately, become somewhat alien. I have the impression that there are two big issues that I focused on when writing them. I am referring to the texts I wrote about what I call the heteronormativity of psychoanalysis. One central theme is eminently political,[6] it refers to heteronormativity and its subjective implications. The other focuses on the strong arguments in psychoanalytic theory to side with the heteronorm. It is about everything that has to do with the articulation of the Oedipus complex with the castration complex. These two central themes are articulated in the clinical proposal to rethink how we theorize and what place we occupy as analysts regarding sexual diversity. The Oedipus reloaded, which I propose, is one reloaded with updates.

Subjective implications of heteronormativity

Reading Foucault, lesbian and gay studies, the queer theory, and some feminist texts allowed me to perceive the enormous importance of the political dimension of sexuality overlooked in most psychoanalytic theories, and try to think about what theoretical, institutional, and clinical effects this omission produces. I would not say that the political dimension of sexuality is completely ignored since it is present in the Freudian texts, but not enough attention is paid to the strength and complexity of heteronormativity defined as a social, political, and economic regime. Most psychoanalytic theorizations are unaware of its importance as a shaper of subjectivities through its complex regulation mechanisms. Moreover, by not reading it, they are part of that regime, without knowing it. I hope I can convey the need to take these devices into account, especially, of course, if we are working with analysands who do not respond in their sexuality (and therefore in their love life) to heterosexuality. It is an aspect of sexuality that does not correspond to the Oedipal, or even to the *psychological*, but which has an enormous impact on subjectivity. I am convinced that if we do not see the importance of this, it is very unlikely that we can be good analysts to the LGBTQI+ people.

Heteronormativity imposes heterosexual practices through various mechanisms, artistic, educational, religious, legal, etc. Our LGBTQI + analysands are *permanently* subject to this type of imposition, it is very important to understand that.[7] In the world that we live in, and thanks to the struggle of many people, our LGBTQI + analysts have a greater chance of resisting it. We have already seen an example of how this imposition of heteronormativity works as the only valid sexuality with Father Patrick's 18 reasons to oppose same-sex marriage. Let us now see two others, one taken from social networks[8] and the other from an online newspaper, to see how the imposition of heterosexuality (often through insult) is articulated with a resistance, which although is sometimes individual, whether it is known or not, is always linked to a collective struggle. I choose these examples, among other things, to show how these mechanisms of power go far beyond the State and the legal order.

First example: taken from a young guy's post who comes from a very small town in the province of La Pampa.[9]

> *"Today I was walking hand in hand with my boyfriend and a couple of guys, on multiple occasions, yelled "FAGGOTS" at us. I was quite disappointed that they took the time to point out something that, in the eyes of anyone, was obvious.*
>
> *When these things happen, I can't help but worry (more) about human idiocy than about homophobia itself. If I'm walking hand in hand with my boyfriend, it's obvious that I've accepted that I'm a fag. I don't know, love yourself and avoid looking like a dumbass. You don't offend me, you don't hurt me, you don't do anything to me.*
>
> *Anyway, these things would horrify me if they came from intelligent people, but since they don't, we continue to brush our beards together. Ohhhh."*

Second example: a letter from journalist Matías Sebastián published on the Cosecha Roja network,[10] addressed to Lionel Messi,[11] in response to the use by the Argentine soccer team of the word "fags" as an insult against journalists who had been critical of the team, in a chant after a win against Ecuador:

> *Dear Messi:*
> *Thank you for so much. We always believed in you. We are filled with joy every time you dribble past the defense of four different players who follow you everywhere on the field and you still pick up your head and go towards the goal.*

That is why we write to you. We wanted to tell you that we weren't the fags who said that you sang the national anthem with your head down. We weren't the fags who demanded that you get your act together because if we didn't go to the World Cup we would lose money. We fags -including those of us who are both journalists and fags!- always knew that you were giving your all on the pitch.

We wholeheartedly cheer you on. We have, dear Messi, a huge heart, which we can look at head on. Being a fag is also brave. Do you remember when you were eleven and they said you weren't going to grow any more? And when you went to Spain when you were barely thirteen?

That tightness in the chest, dear Messi, is what we fags feel when we fall in love with a schoolmate and we become the neighborhood fag. Can you imagine what a kid who is about to come out of the closet feels when his eleven heroes use his identity as an insult?

We fags know, like you, what it means to recover from adversity. The bullying that you received by journalists -they are so macho!- is the same that we receive almost every day of our lives. Sometimes we also dribble past our rivals, but when we pick up our heads the goal is not always there: what we usually see is more and more guys doing the same thing as always; pointing fingers at us, trying to point out his masculinity by making a dent in our bodies.

That is why we write to you, Messi. We could just take the joke and thank you for dedicating the victory to the fag journalists and the whores, but it was not necessary to say all that. Despite the victory, despite the joy, neither the fags nor the whores want anything dedicated to us.

When a public person like you says fag as an insult, the pains of childhood return, when they pointed and then hit you at school. When a person like you says fag it feeds the social macho who kills us, who points to us as if we were the problem when we well know that the problem begins with the machos and their patriarchy.

With all the love we have, Messi: do not use us again to insult anyone. Neither us nor our friends, the whores, who allowed more than one of your desperate teammates to lose their virginity.

For us fags is not an insult. Every year we have a march (to which you are invited whenever you want!) claiming our pride of being fags.

Thank you for so much joy Messi. We will continue to cheer you on wholeheartedly. I hope you celebrate a goal in the final by kissing Pocho Lavezzi.[12]

But beware: we're going to watch this World Cup on TV. There's no chance in hell we're actually going there. In Russia for being a fag they can put you in jail and even kill you. Did you know? I hope you know that, Messi. We love you so much.

Why do I dwell on these examples and not settle for the conceptual definition of heteronormativity and its mechanisms? For something that has quite a bad reputation in the Lacanian sphere: I want you to identify with those gay boys and girls, to put yourselves in the other's shoes, to understand a little more the reality they live, which in certain aspects, is not the one in which most analysts live, at least not analysts who are not lesbians, gays, or anything that does not fit into *straight*. I want them to understand to some extent what it is to be *permanently* subjected to the possibility, or sometimes the reality, of homophobic hostility. I want to convey that homophobic hostility, which is not subjective, *permanently* determines subjectivity, what can be done and what cannot, what can be said and what cannot, and the price that must be paid. I want to emphasize that it is impossible to separate that subjectivity from the effects of these devices, and their possible resistance. Let us take the first example, of the young guy from La Pampa, and let us see in how many aspects his subjectivity and his relationships with others were shaped by all this interplay of power relations that allows those guys to yell at him and his boyfriend, what in a certain sense is evident as the young guy himself says. Of course, yelling "faggots" at them is not simply telling them who they are, it goes much further: it is assigning them an abject place. Those guys do not need any courage to insult gays because the entire regime we are talking about endorses them to do so. More so: it prescribes them to do so.

The young guy from La Pampa, at some point during puberty, like every adolescent whose erotic life is gay, had to accept (but could also have not) that this was his way of living eroticism. If the irruption of sexuality is always terrifying, that terror is multiplied when discovering oneself being what one should not be. When what is wrong is not only what you want but also what you are.[13] Then he had to decide whether or not to express it, whether or not to come out of the closet (and when, where, and with whom), knowing that either of the two decisions (both commanded by the *dispositif* of heterosexuality) would have a high cost. Then he had to decide whether or not he would go out holding hands with his partner in a small town, he had to decide whether he would respond and if so how to the aggressions that he would surely be subjected to. All decisions that, necessarily, were going to affect *the totality* of his relationships: as a son, as a boyfriend, as a friend, as a student, as a partner, as a citizen, eventually as a father, etc. All this in a world in which, due to the struggle of many (I mean, not only for subjective reasons), he was able to come out of the closet or go for a walk hand in hand with his boyfriend, two things unthinkable in not too distant times. As Matías Sebastián rightly says in his letter, being a fag almost forces you to be brave. It is true that the courage of some benefits others.

I once wrote that for analysts, homosexuality is either a pathology (perversion, for example) or it is not an issue, and in this case, the whole issue seems to be dismissed with statements of the kind that anyone, regardless of their anatomy, can be inscribed on either side of the sexuation formulae. It may be true, but if we leave it there, many things are left aside of enormous weight in the life of an LGBTQI+ person. For example, all the decisions that the young guy from La Pampa had to make before writing the post that we discussed. He will continue to face decisions because, at least in the current state of things, coming out never ends, and neither does homophobic violence. So it is not enough for us, analysts, to understand that there is nothing "perverse", nothing "against nature" in other sexualities (assuming that we are on the side of analysts who think like this), it is not enough for us to be politically correct. It is important to see that this is far from exhausting the issue, that an LGBTQI + person has to deal with numerous severe difficulties in their life that are not directly the result of a psychic conflict, but that generate them. You can imagine that the young guy from La Pampa had to go through a lot of anxiety to be able to decide. During this process, he felt fear, had doubts, and was involved, because of his choices, in conflicts of love, loyalties, and fidelities. Gays have sometimes been compared to Jews as a discriminated minority, but there is a very significant difference: in the first instance, Jews rely on their family as a place of containment and support, while many gays continue to be rejected by their own families for being gay (although this is something that, again thanks to the struggle of many, is changing). These are all issues that, if we want to help LGBTQI + analysands, I think it is convenient not to ignore.

Perhaps you are wondering why I am talking about power relations, about heteronormativity, about two kids who are insulted in the street. Are they issues that concern us as analysts? Can we "as analysts" influence the mechanisms of heteronormative power? Would it be appropriate for us to do so? Does that have something to do with our task as psychoanalysts?

Clearly, psychoanalysis is an experience of subjective transformation within the framework of the device established by free association, transference, and interpretation, and which is authorized in an ethic and in a more or less consistent theorization and, more deeply, in the desire of the analyst. In this sense, I am absolutely traditional: psychoanalysis is not a field of political militancy. Although, nothing is left out of politics understood as the sphere of power relations. Betting on the desire of the subject is a policy like betting on the will of God, which we suppose must be Father Patrick's bet. There is no possibility of remaining outside power relations, but there is the possibility of taking a critical position concerning them. Psychoanalysis, by not making a critical reading of the heteronormative regime, was partially absorbed by it (here I would have to make a few disquisitions since there were moments in the history of psychoanalysis in which it was an extremely important element of the normalizing mechanisms and others in which it stood out more, but that exceeds what I propose in this presentation).

I believe that if we do not perceive the enormous incidence of this heteronormative regime with respect to the subjectivity of people who do not respond to heterosexuality, we run the risk of doing what I call *psychologizing*, by which I mean attributing to the subject something that is not subjective. For example, interpreting what the young guy from La Pampa said of him "seeking" this type of aggression, or interpreting the episode as a case of masochism. Or interpret in terms of a demanding superego *all* the difficulties that a gay person goes through in order to express out loud and fulfill their erotic desires and fantasies. Of course, their superego must *also* be taken into account, but it is not the only thing that makes the act of naming themselves and naming their desire difficult. The world, fortunately, is not a mere projection of the fantasies, desires, and constructions of the subject, I suppose that is what Lacan means when he affirms that psychoanalysis is not an idealism. I think that many times disasters are made in the name of the supposed "subjective responsibility". If we want the subject to take responsibility for what does not correspond to them, the only thing we will achieve, if the power of transference is at stake, is producing a superego effect, which will hinder the possibility of them taking charge of their own desires, fears, or limitations. If the psychoanalyst does not distance themself from the *dispositif* of heterosexuality, they are going to reproduce it on the scene of analysis, as I have heard countless times of this happening.

Here is an example, taken from an interview in which Patrick Delaroche[14] offers a clinical vignette[15] of what I call the *psychologizing* of power relations.

> I saw someone for analysis for about ten years who persisted in maintaining multiple relationships with female partners, encountering systematic failure. In that cure, what Freud calls «censorship», that process that is not of the order of repression, but of the *self*-imposed preconscious prohibition, was at the center of the work. He was constrained by the following contradictory imperative: "I desire men, I must desire girls". He told himself that he loved girls, in a dialogue with himself, in the ruminations that are well known in obsessives and thus closed the door to what, for me, in the transference, was evidence: he desired men.

Reading this interpretation, one could imagine that the analysand lives in a world where happily, without any kind of pressure, one can choose to appear to friends, to parents, at work, indistinctly in a relationship with a woman or in a relationship with a man. Which is *just not true*. It was much less so at the time the article was written. If it were true, *coming out* would not exist, nor would the instances of homophobia that I gave you as examples, nor the enormous, immeasurable number that I could continue citing, have been written. The 18 reasons by Father Patrick would not exist. Of course, in some parts of the world, though few, one can appear with a partner of the same sex, but it always means having gone through a more complex and more painful path than the one that heterosexual people have. Reading Delaroche's interpretation, it seems that it is all an intrapsychic issue, of a "*self*-imposed preconscious prohibition", a "dialogue with oneself". It is not like that at all, that is far from being a dialogue with oneself, it is a dialogue with a whole regimen of regulation of sexuality, something that is not in the least a fantasy of the analysand.

Am I saying that there is nothing neurotic about Delaroche's patient? Not at all; that dimension is always there and as analysts it is the one that most interests us, it is the one in which we can operate. However, in order to operate well on the neurosis, it is important to discriminate it from what is not a neurosis. I have the impression that if the treatment had not focused, as Delaroche says, on the supposed *self*-imposed prohibition, it is possible that it would have taken that analysand less time to be able to accept his desire since he could better read what he was facing. Time in life is vital. Delaroche's reading puts all the responsibility on the subject, it is his problem if he cannot choose according to his desire. It is, in my opinion, a reading which puts the blame on the analysand. Of course, no one can prevent an analysand from their own act of assuming what they want (and this is never without anxiety), but homophobia and heteronormativity are not problems that they invent from being neurotic.

This first central theme of the two that I read in my writings on the subject, the political one, tries to situate the regulations of sexuality that go far beyond the narrow horizon of the family. This is without denying the fundamental role played by family ties in the constitution of the subject. The subject is constituted in a field of libidinal forces, giving "libidinal" the meaning of relationships of love, desire, and personalized and nominated jouissance. That libidinal field is provided by the family; a family that is never outside power relations; that is why, rather than "the family", there are families, in the plural. There are poor, rich, foreign, immigrant, Jewish, Christian, Muslim, secular, left-wing, right-wing, blended, single-parent, and dysfunctional families. For some time now, another way of bonding families that has always existed has become visible: homoparental families.

If Father Patricio cares so much about the possibility of homosexual marriage, as he calls it, to the point of accepting what at another time would have seemed to him a complete scandal, the civil union of two women or two men, it is because the homosexual marriage would allow the constitution, or rather the legitimation, of homoparental families. Father Patricio thinks that a child needs a mom and dad. It is the same argument used by some Lacanian analysts in France to oppose the adoption of same-sex couples.

Oedipus complex and castration complex

Indeed, both the Freudian and Lacanian Oedipus are gendered. By "gendered" I mean that they are not only formulated in terms of a father and a mother, a parent of each gender (something completely understandable in the context of the time) but that in their formulation the anatomical sexual difference of the parents plays a fundamental role: the son is desired by the woman as a substitute for the phallus that she does not have, and she looks for it in the man as a substitute for the father who bears the penis. With Freud, this is very clear, however, with Lacan, or in Lacanism (in transmission everything is mixed) this is generally complicated by two statements: that the phallus is not the penis, and that the phallus is a signifier. Although, if it is necessary to clarify that the phallus is not the penis, it is because it has some privileged relationship with the penis, something that Lacan never denies. I give only one quote as proof, (I could give several):

> ...there is someone [the father] who can respond come what may, and who in every case answers that he is the one who's got *the true phallus, the real penis*. He is the one who holds the trump card, and who knows it.
>
> (Lacan, 2020, 201, emphasis mine)

Of course, for the *parlêtre*, the phallus can become the baby, or money, a car, beauty, anything that takes on that *value*, but I refuse, under the banner of the signifier, to reduce the materiality of the bodies to something insignificant. One thing is to say that "phallus" does not have a univocal meaning, and quite another is to claim that the materiality of bodies, including what Freud called the anatomical distinction between the sexes, does not play any role in the constitution of a subject and in the different forms of erotic fantasies.[16]

Homoparental families place a big question mark on the role that anatomical sexual difference plays, or does not play, in the constitution of the subject. It is an experience from which we will learn plenty. To date, all serious studies indicate that the children of same-sex couples do not differ significantly from the children of heterosexual couples. Is it possible that the anatomical sexual difference of the parents, the gender with which they identify, and their choice of sexual object play a lesser role in the identifications and choices of the children than we previously believed?

Here we are getting to the core of the second of the two central themes that I find in my writings. That the Oedipus complex in its articulation with the castration complex has a normalizing function is not something that only Gayle Rubin[17] affirms; Lacan also says so. In his theorization of the Oedipus complex we have a narrative of how the boy becomes a boy, the girl becomes a girl.

> There is, on the other hand, in the Oedipus complex, the subject's assumption of his own sex - that is, to call things by their name, what makes it the case that a man assumes the virile type and that a woman assumes a certain feminine type, recognizes herself as a woman and identifies with her functions as a woman. Virility and feminization are the two terms that translate what is essentially the function of the Oedipus complex. Here we find ourselves at the level at which the Oedipus complex is directly tied to the function of the ego-ideal- it has no other meaning.
>
> (Lacan, 2017, 150)

says Lacan in Seminar V. There are those who are frightened by the idea of "normalizing" something. It is not my case, I see no other alternative but to *try* it, because, as psychoanalysis itself teaches us, there is no natural object for the drive, there is no *natural* sexuality for the *parlêtre*, and it is then what Freud calls "culture" that must offer an object to the drive.[18] That the Oedipus complex states that a normalizing *dispositif* is not, then, in my opinion, the problem itself.[19] The real problem is when psychoanalysis functions as a normalizing *dispositif* for sexuality.

I am guessing that you would like to tell me that this is not the case at all, that psychoanalysis, at least in its Lacanian version, is in no way adaptive, nor is it based on ideals and that it is therefore not suggestive, and will accompany the subject in their desires. Without a doubt that is the spirit of psychoanalysis. However, when it comes to sexualities, psychoanalysis, or perhaps we should say the different types of psychoanalysis, have remained halfway between breaking the ideal mandates and a heteronormative position, no longer based on the same principles as told by Father Patricio, but in a certain reading of some facts of sexual life that are absolutely original to psychoanalysis and that in theory is called the Castration Complex.

The notion of perversion that Freud uses in the famous *Three Essays on the Theory of Sexuality*, from 1905, is taken directly from the psychiatry of the time, it does not arise from psychoanalytic listening, and as Arnold Davidson[20] demonstrates in a brilliant article, it annuls itself when taking into account the revolutionary Freudian affirmation that the sexual drive does not have a natural object. It is contradictory that Freud maintains, in the *Three Essays*, the notion of perversion, since, in 1905, "perversion" takes the meaning of the pathology of an instinct that, as the text itself postulates, does not exist. However, when he formulates the theory of the Oedipus complex, and especially when he articulates it with the castration complex, he can posit a theorization of perversions (and of what Lacan would call sexuation) that is properly psychoanalytic. This is a serious argument and it cannot be taken lightly; although it ends up making a reading of the *other* sexualities not in themselves, but always according to the model of heterosexuality, but this time no longer as the supposed "natural", "normal" sexuality, but as being the only one that recognizes the difference, accepts castration, feminine jouissance, or other similar syntagmas.

As the entire field of other sexualities is varied and complex, and each one has its own specificity, I am going to stick to what I investigated in particular, male homosexuality. In his study of Leonardo, which is where he deals with the subject the most, Freud posits an idea that I believe returns in different forms in many later theorizations, and that I have heard countless times from the mouths of many analysts. It is the idea that homosexuality would be a sort of escape from heterosexuality. He says "By repressing his love for his mother he [the homosexual] preserves it in his unconscious and from now on remains faithful to her" (Freud, 1957 [1910], 100). However, it is important to mention that Freud refers this fixation to the *phallic* mother, the mother endowed with the "distinguishing mark of masculinity" (93) that Freud interprets in the tail of the "vulture" of Leonardo's childhood memory. There is the incidence of the castration complex. The Freudian development says:

> While he seems to pursue boys and to be their lover, he is in reality running away from the other women, who might cause him to be unfaithful. In individual cases direct observation has also enabled us to show that the man who gives the appearance of being susceptible only to the charms of men is in fact attracted by women in the same way as a normal man; but on each occasion he hastens to transfer the excitation he has received from women on to a male object, and in this manner he repeats over and over again the mechanism by which he acquired his homosexuality.
>
> (100)

All this is very surprising! In the first place, as far as I know, no one has such fidelity, not even with their mother. On the other hand, no one flees from a true desire so consistently throughout their life. What does a sexual desire mean that is never conscious, and that would be replaced by another that brings a huge amount of inconvenience to their life? Very bizarre. *In truth*, according to Freud, homosexuals would like women, only they never dare to be unfaithful to the mother, or to deprive the mother of the "distinguishing mark of masculinity". This could make sense if it were proven that after a time of analysis homosexuals overcame their attachment to their mother and discovered their true desire for a woman. However, this is not the case.[21] Freud's theory does not allow him to conceptualize that there is a homosexual object choice, from his point of view, there would only be a permanent escape from the choice of heterosexual object.

You may say that these ideas are from 1910 and that they are already outdated. However, if we take the book of someone who for many of us is a teacher whom we love and respect, and to whom I am in many ways very grateful, Norberto Rabinovich,[22] we will see that on these issues it does not differ so much from the Freudian perspective. In his book *Lagrimas de lo real*, whose first edition is from 2007, that is, a little more than a hundred years after Freud's book, we can read a variant of the same idea. It talks about a concept that in Freud appears related to fetishism and psychosis, but which, seen from the Lacanian perspective, is applied to the field of perversion: "sexual perversions" arise "as a consequence of a marked disavowal of castration, which would arouse in them a fear, at least a little greater than in neurotics." (Rabinovich, 2007, 139).[23] The author takes what he calls "the traditional nosographic classification of sexual perversions" (139), that is, that of psychiatry at the end of the nineteenth century, which defines them by "certain singularities of sexual behavior" (139). In other words, it is not a strictly psychoanalytic classification, but a psychiatric one, and deducing from it, now with concepts of psychoanalysis, a subjective position, that of disavowing castration, which would be corroborated by considering "the salient point that allows to identify more rigorously the perverse cases", that is "the avoidance of heterosexual genital coupling" (139). Of course, according to this reasoning, homosexuality falls squarely into the field of perversion. Due to Norberto being consistent, he includes it among these perverts who would disavow castration. Here we have again, in 2007, the idea that gays do not really like what they think they like but just keep avoiding something else that terrifies them! Curiously, it is an approach that coincides with the premises of heteronormativity, which, as you will remember, considers heterosexuality as the only valid model of sexual-affective relationship. It is not the same, but it is very similar. However, it is not surprising that a theoretical approach that begins in these terms ends in positing that "the pervert fears going to the *predestined* place of sexual coupling" (141). Predestined by whom? Did we not agree, starting with *Three Essays*, that there was no "predestined" object for the drive? With this type of argument we find again, but now in a psychoanalytic theorization, the "perverting the nature of things" of Father Patrick.

This reasoning leads to the idea that the pervert would avoid confronting the failure of the relationship between the sexes. On the contrary, I would believe that if we were to call the harmonious relationship between men and women a "relation between the sexes", it would fail from the start for someone gay; and if we are going to call complementarity of desire and jouissance a "relation between the sexes", gays do not seem much more favored than the rest of humanity in this sense. It must be recognized that, with the honesty that characterizes him, Norberto Rabinovich acknowledges that "according to these theoretical coordinates, sexual desire in the perverse does not differ from that which characterizes the neurotic", that "it is, in principle, a matter of emphasis" (141).

Let us return to Leonardo's article, in which Freud gives another "explanation" of the psychogenesis of homosexuality, an explanation that is at the origin of the ideas that reach Norberto's book. It is the explanation that comes from the castration complex. He takes up ideas that he had stated in his 1908 paper on the sexual theories of children and gives an account of the child's encounter with the anatomical distinction between the sexes, something that for the child was out of his realm of possibility.[24] "He finds that part of his body [the penis] too valuable and too important for him to be able to believe that it could be missing in other people whom he feels he resembles so much". (Freud, 1957 [1910], 95), and in particular in the mother. "This preconception is so firmly planted in the youthful investigator" Freud continues, "that it is not destroyed even when he first observes the genitals of little girls" (95). As you will recall, in the account, the child responds in a strange way confronted with this sinister (*unheimlich*) perception, he does not admit it, but turns a blind eye to it and *disavows* it. Here appears the disavowal referred to the absence of a penis in women. The boy's first reaction, according to Freud, is to affirm that the girl has a penis, except that it is small, but it will grow[25] (a type of argument that will be repeated countless times throughout life, every time one does not want to admit a reality that strongly contradicts an expectation of desire). When verifying that this expectation is not fulfilled in later observations, a new theory appears, articulated by the threat that he has supposedly received: the member was there, but it was cut.[26]

> Under the influence of this threat of castration he now sees the notion he has gained of the female genitals in a new light; henceforth he will tremble for his masculinity, but at the same time he will despise the unhappy creatures on whom the cruel punishment has, as he supposes, already fallen.
>
> (95)

"Before the child comes under the dominance of the castration-complex (...) he still holds women at full value" (96), "often turns into its opposite and gives place to a feeling of disgust which in the years of puberty can become the cause of psychical impotence, misogyny and permanent homosexuality" (96). So the homosexual would supposedly be homosexual because he would never get over this horror of castration.

Let us note that the horror of the female genitalia is not posited by Freud as a feeling characteristic of future homosexuals. On the contrary, he posits it as a universal reaction, in boys, to the discovery of the lack of a penis in women. This horror, according to Freud, has three destinations: impotence, misogyny, and homosexuality. What Freud, as far as I remember, does not clarify is how this horror is overcome. Which brings up another question: what does "overcoming the horror of castration" mean? What does "accepting castration" mean, and in particular, what would it mean on a sexual level? Semantic problems arise from the beginning, because in sexual life, if there was anything to accept, it would be rather that *there is no castration*, castration being a fanciful theory to explain the difference between the sexes, which is what we find. Moreover, what would it mean to accept the difference between the sexes?[27]

This is where I think we may fall into a trap because, in my opinion, the only sign we admit as proof of having "accepted" sexual difference is having chosen it, in the sense that someone with a penis would have "accepted castration" if he wanted someone with a vagina, and vice versa (and this entails a lot, and I mean *lots*, of assumptions). It is quite evident that if we reason like this we slide with astonishing ease toward a heteronormative abyss, since everything that is not the choice of sexual difference, homologated to anatomical sexual difference, is read as a rejection, a disavowal[28] Also, do not tell me that, if you think like this, there will not be a great temptation to try to get the analysand to admit what is supposedly not admitted, to stop rejecting what is supposedly rejected, to stop "disavowing it". This is how we can be embarked, almost without realizing it, on a completely heteronormative direction of the treatment.

I propose that we separate "accepting", "assuming" castration from "choosing" the anatomical sexual difference. In fact, in homosexual choice there is an implicit acceptance of sexual difference since one sex is chosen and not the other. I have the impression that what we call "object choice", which has very little choice, is a very complex process that involves an immeasurable number of variables which in no way can be summed up as whether or not he accepts the lack of the woman's penis. If the supposedly universal horror of the female genitalia of the man is "overcome", and that means that it is accepted that women do not have a penis but do not lack anything, it is possible to think without contradiction that someone accepts it but does not "choose" the woman as an erotic object. Although, if we give "overcoming the horror of castration" the meaning of going from women awakening horror to women awakening desire, it will be because women, for reasons that I believe go beyond any knowledge, were established for that subject as the cause of desire.

I do not believe that the homosexual does not choose the woman because he cannot overcome the horror of the female genitalia. I am not saying that this horror does not exist: some homosexuals, like some heterosexuals, experience it. However, regarding this issue, there is a difference in respect to what happens in heterosexuality that depends on the choice of object: a gay person has fewer reasons than someone heterosexual to "overcome it"[29]; it seems to me that it does not make much sense to overcome horror (in the sense of moving from horror to desire) of something that is not desired.

Notes

1 *Lacantera Freudiana* is a Lacanian psychoanalytic institution, which is based in Argentina and Chile.
2 After a long parliamentary process, the equal marriage project was definitively approved by both chambers of the Chilean Congress on December 7, 2021, and promulgated by the president two days later. The law came into effect on March 10, 2022, thus making Chile the 7th Latin American country and the 31st in the world to have this right for LGTBIQ+ people.
3 Regarding the issue of "gender", feminism, or rather feminism that represents the struggle for the claim of equality. In many ways, psychoanalysis, or rather the various psychoanalytic theories, choose to claim the difference. I believe that the two positions carry a truth, which as we say, could only be half-said. We will have to deal with this irresolvable split.
4 Spanish for "Not one [woman] less". It is a Latin American fourth-wave grassroots feminist movement, which started in Argentina and has spread across several Latin American countries, that campaigns against gender-based violence.
5 I am not referring to the contradictions that may exist *between* the various theories, but to the *internal* contradictions in each theory.
6 It is political, but I always think as an analyst; I am interested in the dimension of power relations (of politics) insofar as it is a producer of subjectivities.
7 This establishes a very different temporality from the oedipal one.

8 It is not by chance that I choose content from social networks. The Internet has enormous potential for possibilities for LGBTQI+ people. As a kid who is gay, trans, etc. you have the choice of not being alone, you can make a community very early thanks to the ease provided by the internet.

9 La Pampa is a province in Argentina.

10 http://cosecharoja.org/messi-los-putos-siempre-te-bancamos/.

11 Lionel Messi is an Argentine professional footballer who plays as a forward for Ligue 1 club Paris Saint-Germain and captains the Argentina national team.

12 Ezequiel (Pocho) Lavezzi is an Argentine former professional footballer who played as a forward.

13 Hence, for LGBTQI+ people, the issue of identity is crucial.

14 Psychiatrist, psychoanalyst, a former member of the Freudian School of Paris.

15 https://sites.google.com/site/olivierdouvilleofficiel/articles/un-mariage-pastout.

16 If it were *only* about the signifier, a transvestite would automatically be a woman when naming herself as such. However, this is not the case, which is why there are still heated discussions on the subject. And this is not the case, among many other reasons, due to the incidence of sexual desire: that the transvestite is a woman with a penis may or may not be a condition of desire. Desire is never politically correct. The anatomy is not insignificant, much less in the erotic life.

17 Rubin, G. (2011). *Deviations*. Durham, NC and London: Duke University Press.

18 For the same reason, I believe that parents who do not want to offer their children neither masculine nor feminine identifications, who look for neutral names and toys, etc., hoping that he or she will "choose" their supposedly spontaneous sexuality, are putting themselves in a very difficult situation. Difficult for their children. There is no desire outside the desire of the Other. Another thing is the cultural redefining of what is masculine and feminine.

19 The problem is, clearly, insisting, as psychoanalysts, on oedipal normalization.

20 Davidson Arnold L., The emergence of sexuality, Harvard University Press, Cambridge Massachusetts, London, England. 2001.

21 As Freud himself admits, for example, in the history of the young homosexual woman, the homosexual desire never disappears and, at the most, can be extended towards heterosexual sexuality. Although, in my experience, the latter never reaches the intensity of desire and enjoyment of the former. It is logical, in the first are the original marks of the constitution of that subject.

22 Norberto Rabinovich is a prestigious Argentine psychoanalyst, and one of the founders of Lacantera Freudiana, where this conference took place.

23 In my opinion, this is an excellent book on the question of jouissance, the best I have read on the subject, but a very retrograde book when it comes to sexuality. A good example of the long-standing contradictions in psychoanalytic theory.

24 Freud makes this account pertaining only to the male child, but since we are now dealing with male homosexuality, it is enough.

25 While I was writing this chapter, I was told about a four-year-old boy who goes into the bathroom while his mother is taking a shower and asks why she doesn't have a dick. Her mother tells him that she has a vagina. The boy, then, responds immediately: "Don't worry mom, it's going to grow up already." In that "don't worry" fits all the anxiety of little Oedipus.

26 I must say that, in my many years of practicing psychoanalysis, I have heard countless times in which someone had reacted with anxiety (usually in childhood) to what was read as the lack of a woman's penis, but I never found the fantasy that "the woman's penis" had been cut off.

27 In other words, some bodies have a penis, others a vagina. I do not delve into the very important issue of intersexuality in this text.

28 A straight man, for example, may want nothing to do with having sex with another man. (in Spanish "not wanting to know" can also mean "does not want anything to do with"), also with a feeling of rejection, without thereby seeing anything pathological in that not wanting to know anything.
29 I am referring specifically to the horror that Freud posits at the basis of homosexuality. The horror of castration, understood as the horror of the loss that desire entails undoubtedly affects us all.

Bibliography

Davidson, A. (2004). *The emergence of sexuality*. Cambridge, MA and London: Harvard University Press.

Foucault, M. (1978). *The history of sexuality, Volume 1: An introduction*. New York, NY: Pantheon Books.

Freud, S. (1975 [1905]). *Three essays on the theory of sexuality*. New York, NY: Basic Books.

Freud, S. (1957). *The standard edition of the complete psychological works of Sigmund Freud, Volume XI (1910)*. London: The Hogarth Press.

Freud, S. (1961). *The standard edition of the complete psychological works of Sigmund Freud, Volume XIX (1910)*. London: The Hogarth Press.

Lacan, J. (2017). *The formations of the unconscious. The seminar of Jacques Lacan, Book V*. Cambridge: Polity Press.

Lacan, J. (2019). *Desire and its interpretation. The seminar of Jacques Lacan Book VI*. Cambridge: Polity Press.

Lacan, J. (2020). *The object relation. The seminar of Jacques Lacan, Book IV*. Cambridge: Polity Press.

Rabinovich, N. (2007). *Lágrimas de lo real*. Rosario: Homo Sapiens Ediciones.

4 Toward a post-heteronormative Oedipus

The crazy love for your father

Alberto is 65 years old, he is a prestigious cardiologist who comes to be analyzed after having read *Oedipus Gay*.[1] He went through various analyses in which his gayness had no place. In some it was directly and crudely pathologized. His analyst, immediately before me, was gay-friendly, that is, he "tolerated" his homosexuality. He even read *Oedipus Gay* when Alberto lent it to him and found it interesting. Even so, he was scared when Alberto wanted to come out of the closet in the academic world, and he strongly advised against it. He told him it would be "sincericide".

Starting from the last years of high school, until he had already graduated as a doctor, Alberto was in love with his schoolmate, Claudio. A friendship that continued through eight turbulent years of Argentine history, from the end of the dictatorship of the Argentine Revolution,[2] going through the democratic presidencies of Héctor J. Cámpora, Raúl Lastiri, Juan Domingo Perón, and Maria Estela Martínez de Perón, until the beginning of the bloody and criminal Process of National Reorganization. Everything seems to indicate that Claudio had feelings for Alberto, but we will never know for sure. We do know that they bathed together, jerked off together, fought naked, slept together, and loved exchanging clothes. Although there was something there, it was not what is called "sex" in the neighborhood.

While the affairs between the two continue, Claudio joins a guerrilla organization with a Marxist-Leninist orientation. Here he becomes involved in the armed struggle, a place to which, despite all his love, Alberto cannot accompany. However, for a time, he acts as a messenger between Claudio, who was living in hiding at the time, and his parents. These are complex years in which some leftist guerrilla organization plants a bomb in Alberto's house, targeting his father, who is a Chief Master Sergeant. Alberto could have been seriously hurt but, fortunately, he is the only one in the house at that time and comes out almost unharmed. The divergent paths that each one is taking progressively distance them. Claudio violently attacks and despises Alberto's "bourgeois" position, who in turn cannot deal with the

DOI: 10.4324/9781003252160-5

suspicion that Claudio has murdered in the name of the revolution. Alberto's love is tainted by anger and resentment.

In February 1978 (while there is a full military dictatorship in Argentina) Claudio is kidnapped by parapolice forces and becomes a missing person (*desaparecido*[3]). In March of the same year Alberto, already graduated as a doctor, enters the army to do compulsory military service as a conscript professional. A small percentage of soldiers would obtain, at the end of a preparatory course, the rank of reserve second lieutenant. Alberto feels so inept for military life that it seems unlikely that he could have been chosen for it. He is now in the army with those who made Claudio disappear, and he has strong reasons to believe that they may have murdered him.[4] In those months Alberto, despite being in love, was very angry with Claudio and among his enemies he was "in the family".

There are many concerns and problems that Alberto is currently facing. However, in this new analysis, he insistently returns to that love, which is presented and arises with the intensity of first love in youth and the added intensity of the unconsummated. This is how he devotes himself to the rewriting of a posthumous letter, which he had written to Claudio, some decades ago. In this dialogue with his absent friend, he tells him that he finally "deserved" to be appointed reserve second lieutenant. Rereading this new version; he is surprised that he used that word. What does it mean that he "deserved it", he wonders now? He evokes, then, his attitude with officers and non-commissioned officers. When they wanted to intimidate and humiliate him, he would make jokes or give them answers that left them bewildered. "Remember my name, because at the end of the summer you are going to hate me, soldier", an officer told him. He answered, with a tone of voice that sounds a mix of innocent and funny: "Do I have to wait until summer?". This provoked a response from the officer that caught my attention: "I can't punish you, soldier". In fact, he was never punished during that course. I keep listening to Alberto and I realized: that he addresses the officers without fear, as if they could not intimidate him. Let us remember that his father, and many other members of his family, were a part of the armed forces.

Trying to understand the enigmatic reason why he "deserved" to be among those chosen as a reserve second lieutenant, he remembers the shooting test. He hates guns. He remembers with horror the outings with his father and brother to shoot foxes or hares when they had transferred his father to Patagonia. Although, when it was his turn to shoot during the tests, it was as if something inexplicable possessed him, and he passed the test with flying colors. He received a very high score.

As Alberto rightly says, he charmed military men, that is, the torturers and possible murderers of Claudio, but also his father's comrades-in-arms. It is possible that fear played a part and that charm was a sort of survival tactic for him. Although, the whole context of the associations, which I do not know if I managed to convey well, indicates that there is more to it than that. "It's the crazy love for your father", I tell him. "Crazy" because in a rational and conscious sense Alberto certainly did not love him. More importantly, he was not an affectionate father to him (as he was to his brother, who is now a Chief Master Sergeant). One time, I think when he was eight or nine years of age, Alberto got mad at his father and stopped talking to him for about two years. Alberto, years later realized his father had not even noticed that they had stopped talking. I tell him that it seems to me that it is the crazy love for his father that makes him charm military men, that something of the most unconscious bond with his father possessed him when they put a rifle in his hands. He responds with an association that seems to me to confirm the interpretation: when he was appointed reserve second lieutenant, he ran happily to tell his father. Being among those as a reserve sub-lieutenant evidently had the unconscious significance of being, at last, chosen by his father. The father who had always chosen his brother and who did not notice that Alberto had not spoken to him for two years. Many decades later, he would dare to give up his post at an armed forces hospital but only after his father passed away.[5]

I was interested in this clinical vignette for several reasons. First, because the associations begin with Alberto's surprise. That function of surprise is so central in analysis. I would say that any analysis without the element of surprise in both the analysand and the analyst is not going to work. When Alberto is surprised by the word "deserved" he is already outlining a reading, that word is suddenly imbued with nonsense, with something enigmatic that questions him and invites him to decipher. The suspicion is installed that this word is the index of something still unknown. The connection with the Oedipal is not immediately seen, there is even something in Alberto's conscious attitude toward the military men that goes in the opposite direction. Rather he would tend to downplay that promotion. As soon as he associates, another enigmatic fact appears: the shooting test, in which, once again, he appears to be someone other than the one he believes to be. Someone who hates weapons makes a brilliant shooting test, someone who would downplay having been promoted to reserve second lieutenant writes that it was a merit that he hastens to offer to his father. In both cases, he appears to be much closer to his father than might be supposed from their relationship and conscious memories of him. What father is this to whom he is close, to whom he dedicates his promotion? Is it the father he really had, or is he the one he longed to have? I would say that he is the Oedipal father, understanding as such the father who is forged from childhood desires and passions, in a certain sense a father who never existed, but who has complex and indiscernible links with the person who entered him into the registry office and who took him hunting in Patagonia.

I also like this clinical vignette because it illustrates very clearly that this dimension of Oedipal love is radically unconscious, it is situated, according to the beautiful metaphor that Freud takes from Fechner, in "another scene", and contradicts the representations that each one has of themself. Yet, or for that very reason, it has a very powerful impact on

the life of each one. In themselves, moreover, oedipal loves have no established link to sexual choice or sexual identity. If I chose, among so many
other vignettes that I could have opted for, one of a man who falls in love
with other men, it is precisely to underline that this oedipal dimension that
exists completely independent of how each one desires and loves. It has
no necessary relationship with any device of good sexuation. Rather than
proposing to get rid of the Oedipus complex, as a gay person I would propose the opposite: we are as oedipal as anyone. Being gay (or lesbian, or
queer, or trans) does not mean being outside the oedipal because no one
is constituted outside the field of the Other's desire. The founding times
leave indelible marks on any subjectivity which has a force that is not comparable to any other. It is different when the good and bad ways of going
through Oedipus are established, as they were established in the history of
psychoanalysis. There, I believe, is the problem, and not in the very notion
of the Oedipus complex.

Finally, I also chose this vignette because it shows very clearly that the
oedipal is never restricted to the family sphere, that history and its din run
through it.

Shibboleth

The oedipal became synonymous with the conservative established order,
patriarchal and heteronormative. It is held responsible for throwing into
abjection bodies and subjectivities that do not respond to compulsory heterosexuality. Gayle Rubin says that "In the most general terms, the Oedipal complex is a machine which fashions the appropriate forms of sexual
individuals" (Rubin, 2018, p. 40). If there are appropriate forms of sexual
individuals, there would have to be other inappropriate ones. Unsuccessful
and failed forms. Many psychoanalysts seem to think and intervene in that
manner. In an interview in the newspaper El País,[6] Élisabeth Roudinesco
told the journalist that 70% of French analysts opposed same-sex marriage
on the grounds that it would be "contrary to the Oedipus complex".

How did the Oedipus complex go from being the bearer of the horror that
sullies infantile purity, the same one that pushes Oedipus to gouge out his
eyes, to being the regulator of the normality of bodies and desires? What
happened to the horror of the mother who finds out that, with her care,
she awakens the sexual drive of her son?[7] Would the Oedipus complex have
ceased to be the *shibbolet* that separates supporters and opponents of psychoanalysis, to become its rejection in the new *shibbolet* that separates a
reactionary and heteronormative psychoanalysis from one that is renewed
and open to new bodies and sexualities?

I have insistently maintained, and have argued in different ways in this
book, that a certain way of reading the articulation of the Oedipus complex
with the castration complex has become the heteronormative *dispositif* par
excellence of psychoanalysis. Along with the same perseverance, I have been
saying that the Oedipus complex is not only that. I would even go so far as

to say that essentially, at least what I would call the Oedipus complex, it is not that. Let us return to the *shibboleth*, to what Freud considered the distinguishing mark of the psychoanalyst. He writes in a footnote to the third of the *Three Essays on the Theory of Sexuality*, the one dealing with *The Metamorphoses of Puberty*, that "With the progress of psycho-analytic studies the importance of the Oedipus complex has become more and more clearly evident; its recognition has become the shibboleth that distinguishes the adherents of psycho-analysis from its opponents" (Freud, 1975 [1905], 92). What is this "importance" of the Oedipus complex? Let us put this statement in context. The paragraph where the quote appears begins like this:

> It has justly been said that the Oedipus complex is the nuclear complex of the neuroses and constitutes the essential part of their content. It represents the peak of infantile sexuality, which, through its after-effects, exercises a decisive influence on the sexuality of adults. Every new arrival on this planet is faced by the task of mastering the Oedipus complex; anyone who fails to do so falls victim to neurosis.
>
> (92)

Clearly, this is not about the canonical way of being a man or a woman, but about the influence of infantile sexuality on adult sexuality and the danger of falling into that sort of ordinary unhappiness that we call neurosis.

The footnote is found in Chapter 5 of the essay, titled *The Finding of Object*. This chapter is about the passage from a predominantly autoerotic sexuality to the enjoyment of another body. A passage that has a stopover in the development of fantasy. The great affirmation of this chapter is: "The finding of an object is in fact a refinding of it" (88). Something that had already been pointed out by writers and poets, but that in the Freudian narrative is articulated in a novel way to the symptom and the neurosis. At the very start, the sexual drive had an object "outside the infant's own body" (99), imagined in the maternal breast, which is lost in order to later try to rediscover it, various metamorphoses through, in other(s) body(s), which will never be *that one*.

In the same chapter there is another narrative of the origin of sexuality that allows a richer reading of what is heard in the clinic since it is not only about the child and the breast (the subject and the object), but about what we could call the intertwining of desires:

> A child's intercourse with anyone responsible for his care affords him an unending source of sexual excitation and satisfaction from his erotogenic zones. This is especially so since the person in charge of him, who, after all, is as a rule his mother, herself regards him with feelings that are derived from her own sexual life: she strokes him, kisses him, rocks him and quite clearly treats him as a substitute for a complete sexual object.
>
> (89)

It is not only about the child's desire and excitement, but also about the desire and jouissance of the person who cares for them, and who by caring for them libidinizes them as well. Although Freud does not manage to state it explicitly in those terms, this narrative allows us to think that the subject's desire to come does not spring from any interiority, but from his encounter with the desire of others,[8] and will forever bear the marks of that origin. This intertwining of desires is the core of what I would continue to call Oedipus, and that is not to be confused with a device to adequately form erogenous bodies.

The *refinding of the object*, which the chapter deals with, is a very special one because the object is reencountered, but in another. *The Self and the Other*, like the beautiful title of a book by Borges. Between finding and refinding, the barrier of incest, that is, social thirdness.

> Respect for this barrier is essentially a cultural demand made by society. Society must defend itself against the danger that the interests which it needs for the establishment of higher social units may be swallowed up by the family; and for this reason, in the case of every individual, but in particular of adolescent boys, it seeks by all possible means to loosen their connection with their family - a connection which, in their childhood, is the only important one.
>
> (Freud, 1975 [1905], 91)

In the sphere of family ties, the *infans* receives a libidinal bath that will shape the unpredictable paths that his eroticism will take. Although the family, to the extent that it is traversed by the institutions and apparatus of society, is also one who conveys the prohibition that relaunches each one, to some extent, beyond the family, into social circulation. The concept of "Oedipus complex" includes the double and contradictory movement of libidinization and prohibition. In this sense, the Oedipus complex and its resolution would name the possible modalities in the passage from the family to society, and the neuroses would be the different ways of being stuck. I would also point out that this passage is always dirty, and that the tension between desire and prohibition is never clearly resolved. What is most properly psychoanalytic is not to point out the importance of the incest barrier (anthropology had already done that), but to affirm that this barrier does not annul desire. "Psychoanalytic investigation shows, however, how intensely the individual struggles with the temptation to incest during his period of growth and how frequently the barrier is transgressed in phantasies and even in reality" (Freud, 1975 [1905], 91). This is the only way to explain a truly scandalous statement, which always surprised me that it is rarely quoted (as if it is preferred to avert the eyes from what it implies):

> It sounds not only disagreeable but also paradoxical, yet it must nevertheless be said that anyone who is to be really free and happy in love

must have surmounted his respect for women and have come to terms
with the idea of incest with his mother or sister.

(Freud, 1957 [1910], 186)

In this sentence, the Oedipus complex recovers all its political incorrectness, and far from being the machine for modeling appropriate forms of
individuals, it is a reading of the drive that is not subordinated to the ideal.
It makes room for the disagreeable and the paradoxical, for the desire that
overcomes respect and horror. That is the aspect of the theorization of the
Oedipus complex that I do not want to lose. Of course, this entire narrative
in Freud's text is crossed by heteronormative perspectives (the chapter of
Three Essays that we are commenting on ends in a section on *Prevention
of Inversion*) and patriarchal perspectives (generally the narrative is made
from the point of view of the male), but in no way do I think that it is only
a patriarchal and heteronormative narrative. Let us not throw the baby out
with the bathwater!

If it is named "complex" it is because it is a knot in which many strings
are tied together: characters, desires, bodies, fears, expectations, loves, ri-
valries, hostility, threats, body parts, guilt, hate, disappointment, envy, etc.
It is also a task. Freud says it clearly in the paragraph we mentioned above:
"Every new arrival[9] on this planet is faced by the task of mastering the Oedipus complex; anyone who fails to do so falls a victim to neurosis" (Freud,
1975, 92). What would the "mastering" of the Oedipus complex consist of,
and what would "resolving" it mean? There is a way of approaching the resolution that is present in Freud, and that was very preponderant in certain
post-Freudian psychoanalysis, in which to dominate Oedipus is to reach
heterosexual genital maturity. Throughout this book, I have taken the time
to show some of the theoretical key concepts, and the violence that this version meant for many people. However, in the same chapter of *Three Essays*,
there is another narrative about the task presented by the Oedipus complex,
which is that "At the same time as these plainly incestuous phantasies are
overcome and repudiated, one of the most significant, but also one of the
most painful, psychical achievements of the pubertal period is completed:
detachment from parental authority (...)" (Freud, 1975 [1905], 93). This articulation is key, it clarifies that the oedipal journey it is not only about sexuality and aggressiveness but also about power. The neuroses, in this sense,
will be the various ways of failing in the task of becoming independent from
the authority (the desire) of the parents.

Men are useless

Mirtha is 55 years old. She is married to Juan and they have three children.
She is a teacher. She starts the analysis by saying "I want to talk about my
mother, it is my central theme". It could be said that she lives in Buenos
Aires to be away from her mother. "My mother despised my father; she
thinks that men are useless".[10] Surely the immediate trigger for the demand

for analysis was the acceleration of the signs of deterioration of her mother, who at this point is a woman of almost 90 years. "I can't handle that, I can't lose her. If she passes away, I feel like I lose a fundamental part of me, she is what sustains me". Mirtha regrets that her mother has not allowed her to have a relationship with her father. At the beginning of her marriage, Mirtha treated Juan with the same contempt with which her mother treated her father. She sometimes believes that Juan looks like her father, which she admits is objectively not true. I tell her that desire slips into this confusion (the refinding of the object). She rejects that possibility, but she associates that in the sexual act she is horrified to see Juan's face. This only happens after her marriage, before she enjoyed sex a lot, with Juan or with previous partners. Although, before her marriage, her mother was not aware of her sexual and emotional life. "I'm afraid of my mom. That they'll tell me I'm not behaving properly. That they'll accuse me in front of my mother that I experience pleasure".

Although, in a certain sense, Mirtha has become independent from her parents, has started a family, raised children, and has had a successful career, in another respect she continues to be under the authority of her mother (she is afraid that she will be accused of wrongdoing in front of her). When she, at 55 years old, can speak with the freedom that the framework of psychoanalysis gives, the theme that emerges immediately and in an absorbing way is her relationship with her mother, which is really her relationship with her parents. Her mother's contempt for her father[11] marks her subjectivity, which becomes evident when she chooses to talk about that topic to present herself in her first session; or when she repeats that behavior on getting married herself. It is evident that the latter cannot be understood only from Mirtha's bond with Juan, it is the history of the bond between her parents that determines it. Although that contempt, added to the horror, also makes evident her childhood love for her father. A love that, as Freud stubbornly maintains, is also sexual. Contempt for men (for the father) is not the opposite of desire, but its reverse. Mirtha as a child read likely read behind her mother's contempt for her father, and for men in general, a desire that perhaps made her feel despised. Mirtha also allows us to understand that the "oedipal" mother is not the actual mother (Mirtha is far away from her real mother, with the oedipal she is in a sort of symbiosis), that the actual father is not the father of her erotic desire (the first one brings up feelings of tenderness within her as he quietly tolerates his wife's contempt, the second provokes when she refinds him in Juan, an arousal that horrifies her. At least under her mother's gaze). I cannot find a better way to name this intertwining (which has nothing to do with good or bad sexuation, but with desire, excitement, anxiety, and symptoms) other than "oedipal".

Sandro's[12] girlfriend

In general, the Oedipus complex is theorized (or criticized) based on the texts on sexuality that Freud wrote starting with the famous article on *The infantile genital organization*, from 1923. Articles in which what will be called sexuation are at the center of Freud's theorizing. However, he was not trying to explain why someone became a man or a woman as he realized the importance of the Oedipus complex. The road was very different. In the investigation of inhibition, symptom and anxiety, and in listening to his patients, Freud comes across relationships intensely charged with affects (of all kinds of affects), desires, aggression, valuations, promises of hierarchies, mandates, ideals, and libido between parents and children. The same path by which he arrives at the notion, so closely linked to that of the Oedipus complex, of an infantile sexuality that leaves indelible marks, and that exploits the multiple possibilities of the erogenous body to obtain pleasure. Along this path, he comes across a complex set of desires and ideals that circulate between parents[13] and children. In this sense, the Oedipus complex would be like the navel that remains in the psyche due to the fact of not having given birth to itself, of the radical impossibility of the *self-made man*. What makes the relationship with parents (regardless of whether it is good, bad, lousy, whether one stays attached to them, separates on good terms, or lives to escape from them), insofar as they are the people who provide us with support (*holding*, as Winnicott would say) essential to avoid succumbing to helplessness, not comparable to any other relationship.

Coincidentally, while I was ruminating on these ideas, I found a clear way to illustrate this privileged place of parents in the subjectivity of each one, which I did not take from the clinic, but from a podcast with Camila Sosa Villada, an Argentine writer and actress. In the podcast *La cruda*, hosted by Migue Granados,[14] she speaks on the moment when she went from working as a prostitute to fame. Her rise comes from the play, *Carnes Tolendas*, in which she acts, and which includes testimonies of her own life as a transvestite (the subtitle of the play is *Scenic Portrait of a Transvestite*). The journalist asks her if she had felt ashamed of practicing prostitution and she replies:

> Selling ice cream was worse, seeing my mother cleaning other people's houses was worse, crying because the bosses mistreated her, cleaning the pension in which I lived to be able to pay the rent was worse (...) I felt embarrassed when I started to be known. This started in 2009, I starred in a play called *Carnes Tolendas*. I also had a blog called *Sandro's girlfriend*, and there I sometimes told things that happened to me with clients, I also uploaded photos of myself fucking. When I started to become famous, I said: "my dad and my mom can't know this, they can't know that I did this." I felt embarrassed for them.

Of course, one can appeal to a certain way of theorizing the Oedipus complex to "explain" why Camila Sosa Villada is a transvestite – what failure, what deviation, what disavowal of reality lies in that stubborn identity. It is the narrative of good and bad Oedipus, of finished versions and truncated ones. This entire book opposes that reading. Although, without knowing anything more about Camila's subjectivity, from what she says about shame, one can affirm that for her the gaze of the parents is distinguished from any other gaze and that before that gaze, just like Mirtha before the "gaze" of her mother wants to erase the traces of her desire.[15] She can show her desire to the rest of the world, but not to her parents.[16] If we could continue the dialogue with Camila, within the framework of analysis, we would find that the same desires that she wants to erase are intertwined with the wishes and expectations of her parents in complex, unpredictable ways that are impossible to fully unravel. We would also see that this plot occupies a privileged place both in what becomes symptomatic and in what becomes sublimations and fantasies of desire. I find no reason not to continue calling this whole framework an "Oedipus complex". It is true that my definition is more encompassing than what Freud calls the Oedipus complex because it is not limited to the phallic phase, but encompasses the entire subtle fabric of desires (it is a simplification, but I hope it is understood) that is concocted from before the birth of a subject. Let us say that I do not distinguish oedipal from pre-oedipal, precisely because the idea of pre-oedipal is part of a normative modality of reading what I would continue to call Oedipus.

I do not know if it works like this in all cultures, my knowledge is not that vast. I suppose that there will be significant differences depending on the type of upbringing, the kinship structure, and in more comprehensive terms, the different forms of exercising and structuring of power in societies. In all cultures the *infans*, and for many years, requires adults who are willing to take care of themselves so that they can survive, name themselves, discover the world, love and be loved, find some identity, access an erotic life, etc. However, this happens and it has important consequences for everyone. In no culture does anyone birth themself. The human animal does not humanize itself and culture is not an abstraction, it is always incarnate.

Queer psychoanalysis

In the excellent book, *Queer psychoanalysis*, Fabrice Bourlez asks "how to go beyond Oedipus?" (Bourlez, 2021, 49). In this sense, Oedipus is presented as something which must be overcome. What does "Oedipus" mean in Bourlez's book? At first, to sign "an adherence to the traditional father-mother-baby family structure" (51), and oppose, as pathological and contrary to the "civilizing order", the other variants of family structure and kinship. Clearly, if that is Oedipus, *we must* go further, that is what this book is also about.

Bourlez cites the letter in which Freud informs Fliess of the discovery of the Oedipus idea and places there the germ of the universalization of a family and upbringing model.

> One single thought of general value has been revealed to me. I have found, in my own case too, falling in love with the mother and jealousy of the father, and I now regard it as a universal event of early childhood, [...] If that is so, we can understand the riveting power of Oedipus Rex....
> (Freud, 1966 [1886–1899], 265)

No doubt this can be read quite literally, as every boy falls in love with his mother and is jealous of his father. It can even be read, and has been read, not as a description of a situation but as a prescription: that must be the family structure and that is how desire must be channeled. However, what happens if we read it in another way, and do not locate what is universal in the heterosexual mom-dad-son family structure, but in the fact that primary relationships (whatever they may be) are deeply eroticized from the outset, crossed by strong and contradictory affects, and that leave indelible marks on subjectivity? If we read it that way, we are not proposing any idea about what sexuality, sexual identity, or family formation should be.

Commenting on Deleuze and Guattari's *Anti-Oedipus*, Bourlez uses a quote from the first appearance of Oedipus (not yet named as a complex) in a printed work. In *The Interpretation of Dreams*, Freud writes that the "profound and universal power to move [of Sophocles' tragedy] can only be understood if the hypothesis I have put forward in regard to the psychology of children has an equally universal validity" (Freud, 1953 [1900], 261). This is exactly the universal validity of "this little oedipal theater" (Bourlez, 2021, 62) which is questioned both by Fabrice and by "theories that deconstruct the genre" (62). "In fact", continues Bourlez, "strictly considered from the perspective of the Oedipus complex, the *talking cure* ends up becoming an old morality". This undoubtedly happens when the authentically analytical position is lost, and a certain way of understanding Oedipus becomes a model for what it should be, and what it should be for everyone, universally. Although, again, is that what we find in the text from Freud from which the quote was taken?

In principle, let us remember that this first appearance of Oedipus in a publication does not take place in a chapter about the norms of healthy sex, the correct ways of being a man or a woman, or forming a family. It is not about determining the "normality" of the subject, but about *Dreams of the Death of whom the Dreamer is Fond*. We know that Freud's interpretation is that these dreams carry a death *wish* toward loved ones. Something that does not seem very consistent with any morality. Freud himself is led to begging his readers to listen "Before this idea is rejected as a monstrous one..." (Freud, 1953 [1900], 256). If the idea of a death *wish* directed at loved ones is monstrous, how much more so is its corollary, the idea that the death wish is linked to an incestuous desire. "None of the findings of psycho-analytic research has provoked such embittered denials, such fierce opposition..." (263), Freud comments in a 1914 footnote. Far from debuting as a prescription of what healthy sex should be, Freud proposes that we pay attention, in this section, to something that we would prefer not to look at because it would violently contradict ideals culturally invested with great sacredness.[17] "Like Oedipus, we live in ignorance of these wishes, repugnant to morality (...)". (263) In what I consider a genuinely analytical position, Freud invites us to go beyond the idealized vision of what the world should be and put up with some truths that can be disturbing.

Before this idea is rejected as a monstrous one, it is as well in this case, too, to consider the real relations obtaining - this time between parents and children. We must distinguish between what the cultural standards of filial piety demand of this relation and what everyday observation shows it in fact to be. More than one occasion for hostility lies concealed in the relation between parents and children (...) The sanctity which we attribute to the rules laid down in the Decalogue has, I think, blunted our powers of perceiving the real facts.

(256)

Freud does not fail to point out that the very structure of the bourgeois family of his time, and the place that the father occupied in it, even encouraged the hostility and death wish of the son.

There is, then, a version of the Oedipus complex, which is the original formulation of the Freudian experience, which, far from being a normalizing *dispositif*, is the unveiling of a truth that is initially horrifying and repulsive. In this sense, Freud would be an Oedipus who decides not to gouge out his eyes, but to look squarely at the truth of his desire and decipher an enigma more fearsome than the one the Sphinx had proposed to him. A truth that, far from being constituted as morality, threatens morality and good customs. An analysand told me that she had feared that I would interpret the dream that she spoke about to reveal that she wanted her father dead. Obviously, that was the desire of the dream, and to position oneself as an analyst is to confront the subject with those desires, not to stupidly reassure her.

When Ernst Lanzer, known in the history of psychoanalysis as "the rat man", describes his criminal impulses and self-reproaches, Freud does not reassure him (as Ernst's best friend unsuccessfully tried), assuring him that he is blameless, but rather aimed directly at confronting him with his desire to murder his father. That this wish was addressed to a father who at that point was already dead nine years earlier clearly indicates to us (as in Mirtha's story, or Alberto's) that this murder takes place in "another scene", but not without profound and complex consequences on Ernst's life and relationships. The development of his clinical history makes it clear that "carrying it out" is not what must be avoided, but rather it is necessary so that Ernst can, as we saw what Freud proposed above, get rid of the authority of the parents.

Fabrice Bourlez is not unaware of this other version of Oedipus, although he prefers to reserve the name "Oedipus complex" for the one that was created, within psychoanalytic theory and institution itself, as a way of justifying and prescribing the established order. With this version, says Fabrice, certain psychoanalysts "endorse their enduring belief in an order and in a thought that we would have difficulty qualifying in any other way than through the term *straight*, typical of the novelist and post-feminist theorist Monique Wittig" (51). Fabrice affirms that the "Adherence to the Oedipus complex, to the most hackneyed version of it, is the very pillar of this thought (...)". (52) It is for this version of Oedipus, the pillar of heterosexual thought, that Fabrice decides to reserve the name "Oedipus complex". Although, he is not unaware that there are others, as he demonstrates when he clarifies that it would be "the most hackneyed version of it".

What I would continue calling the "Oedipus complex", separating it from the hackneyed version, is touched on in his text. On page 106, he says that

> Psychoanalysis is not the instrument of normalization of minor peoples.[18] It should not propose to cure them of anything, more modestly, it should propose a listening that will allow the subject to express their existence not only based on sociological, ideological or political determinants, nor only based on dominations and injustices that they have received throughout their life. Yet, based on the way they have lived it in their own body and how they can put it into words. In other words, to see what the mark of the Other (social, family, language) is made of in their body and to grasp its irreducibility.
>
> (106)

It is this irreducible mark of the familiar Other (which is the area where both language and the social relations that cross it are transmitted) that I continue to call the Oedipus complex.

Later, he says that in an analytical journey, "at every step we perceive that it is always possible to invent answers or alternatives to what the Other, the family destiny, the anamnestic coordinates, have imposed on us" (140). That family destiny, those anamnestic coordinates, are closely linked to what I would continue to call the Oedipus complex. Dialoguing with Judith Butler, Fabrice affirms that: "we cannot obtain, through consciousness or language, total control over those primary relationships of dependency that make us impressionable, that form and constitute us in a dark and persistent way". (189); and a little further down,

> Indeed, the dependency on the Other and the hole at the base of the narrative of the self are rooted in the mystery of our own sexual origin, whatever it may have been. The link with a lineage that has preceded us – even the most *queer* – implies a link with the Other and therefore marks the evident absence of any possibility of self-engendering. Since I was not born of myself, I depend on the Other, and since I depend on the Other, I suffer from a lack of complementarity in my Self.

The close link between these paragraphs and what I have been proposing in this chapter as the Oedipus complex beyond its heteronormative and prescriptive version is evident. Both Fabrice and I are sensitive to those "primary relationships of dependency that make us impressionable, that form and constitute us in a dark and persistent way". In fact, I think that anyone who goes through the analytic experience develops sensitivity to the enormous importance of these relationships. The clarification that Fabrice makes is very important when he says that they form and constitute us in a *dark* and *persistent* way, or when he points out *the mystery of our own sexual origin*. In this way, he preserves a fundamental non-knowledge, essential to avoid falling into the temptation, so easy, of filling it with good sex techniques. Those dependencies, those lineages, even the most *queer*, constitute us, but we can never reach the formula that encrypts our sexual being, nor is it necessary. It is more about seeing what can be done with it.

Why do I prefer to keep the name "Oedipus complex"? In principle because I see no reason not to keep it. As I hope to have shown in this chapter, it is a way of theorizing that undoubtedly originates from Freudian discovery. This version of Oedipus that I propose is not normative at all, although, as I hope to have shown in this book, it was entangled from the beginning in the *dispositifs* of heterosexuality. There is a revulsive and distressing dimension of existence to which Freud does not retreat, and which is largely concentrated in that central notion of the Oedipus complex. The theorization of Oedipus preserves the division of the subject, the drive dimension, and with it the edge of the truly unconscious. It reminds us of the central role of childhood sexuality far beyond childhood.

When Fabrice Bourlez proposes "Considering Oedipus no longer as a universal but as a possible passage, at a given moment, for the constitution of subjectivity" (72), he is referring to the hackneyed version of Oedipus. Being dependent on the Other (whatever configuration it takes) and being deeply marked by its desire is not a possible passage, but a necessary condition. That is why I would not propose, like Fabrice, a post-oedipal psychoanalysis but a post-heteronormative Oedipus.

Notes

1 In the Spanish edition, the title of this book was *Oedipus Gay* and its subtitle was *Heteronormativity and Psychoanalysis*.
2 The Argentine Revolution is the name given to the civic-military dictatorship that overthrew constitutional President Arturo Illia through a coup on June 28, 1966. The "Argentine Revolution" did not present itself as "provisional" as in all the previous coups, but instead sought to establish itself as a new permanent dictatorial system. Its rule lasted until 1973.
3 Detenido desaparecido or Detenidos desaparecidos (DD. DD.) is the name commonly used in Latin American countries to refer to victims of kidnapping, usually taken to clandestine detention centers and tortured, and crimes of forced disappearance, committed by various authoritarian military dictatorships during the 1970s and 1980s, and officially recognized, among others, by the governments of Argentina (1984) and Chile (1991), etc.
4 Supposedly Claudio was murdered in June 1978, when Alberto was already working as a doctor in the army, but he learned that many years later.
5 While he was in his position at that hospital, Alberto never "thought" not to resign so as not to upset his father. This could only be read après-coup. That he did not resign shows the strength of the oedipal love for his father, that he did not think about it makes us take the word "unconscious" seriously.

6 https://elpais.com/cultura/2015/09/02/babelia/1441210297_491115.html.
7 "A mother would probably be horrified if she were made aware that all her marks of affection were rousing her child's sexual instinct and preparing for its later intensity". (Freud, 1975 [1905], 89).
8 The expression, "the desire of the Other", in the singular, is a simplification that is justified when we talk about the important role that the mother usually plays in raising the child. Even if we limit ourselves to that relationship, it is a misleading simplification, because the mother is always caught, like everyone else, in a network of desires.
9 This is universally problematic, of course. I do not think that this way of thinking about the Oedipus complex can be transposed to any other culture. I even doubt that it can be applied, without profound modifications, at all levels of this culture. Although, here I also reach the limit of my knowledge. I believe that the concept of the Oedipus complex has full meaning only in the field of the experience of analysis, so I am content to offer my version of how I understand it in the culture in which I practice.
10 This lack of contempt for men is due to multiple factors, it cannot be attributed solely to subjective causes. Mirtha's maternal lineage comes from a violently macho and highly racist cultural context.
11 The mother, of course, is a divided subject, and that contempt did not prevent her from entering a long and deep depressive crisis when she separated from her father.
12 Sandro was an extremely popular Argentine singer of slow ballads, rock and roll, and pop. He acted as well.
13 I use "parents" in a very broad sense, to refer to the people in charge of raising the child, regardless of the number of parents or gender.
14 https://open.spotify.com/episode/2ToYOVMdrjOlkdugdBAI6z?si=06f03b7ab-c3b4a86.
15 A situation that I have repeatedly encountered in the clinic and in life is that of someone who has come out in all significant areas of their life, except to their parents. As a general (not universal) rule, coming out to parents is the most difficult and most significant step. Another example of that privileged place that parents have in subjectivity.
16 In reality, it is not so much the gaze of the parents as people, but rather their internalization in that agency that Freud called the superego. However, for each one, the two things are intertwined.
17 Of course, the psychoanalytic discourse and institution pushed the boundaries of what is thinkable and admissible, and today there are those who would not be horrified by the idea that there are death wishes directed towards loved ones, or incestuous wishes for that matter. However, this acceptance is more apparent than real, the drive continues to produce rejection, even in progressive discourses.
18 Bourlez calls "minor peoples" all those who are not installed in the centrality of power.

Bibliography

Bourlez, F. (2021). *Queer psicoanálisis/queoír psicoanálisis*. Argentina: Artefactos (no English translation).
Freud, S. (1975 [1905]). *Three essays on the theory of sexuality*. New York, NY: Basic Books.
Freud, S. (1953). *The standard edition of the complete psychological works of Sigmund Freud, Volume IV (1900)*. London: The Hogarth Press.

Freud, S. (1957). *The standard edition of the complete psychological works of Sigmund Freud, Volume XI (1910)*. London: The Hogarth Press.

Freud, S. (1961). *The standard edition of the complete psychological works of Sigmund Freud, Volume XIX (1923–1925)*. London: The Hogarth Press.

Lacan, J. (2002). *Ecrits*. New York, NY and London: W. W. Norton & Company.

Lacan, J. (2017). *The formations of the unconscious. The seminar of Jacques Lacan, Book V.* Cambridge: Polity Press.

Lacan, J. (2019). *Desire and its interpretation. The seminar of Jacques Lacan Book VI.* Cambridge: Polity Press.

Lacan, J. (2020). *The object relation. The seminar of Jacques Lacan, Book IV.* Cambridge: Polity Press.

Wittig, M. (1992). *The straight mind*. Boston, MA: Beacon Press.

II
Miscellanea

5 On the political incorrectness of eroticism

This chapter, which navigates between politics and jouissance like the rest of the book, is the only one that is not directly about heteronormative dispositfs and their effects on psychoanalytic theory itself. However, it seemed important to include this because it deals with something that is preserved in psychoanalytic discourse and accounts for what is at the core of the rejection of eroticism that is expressed as heteronormativity. This would be the subject of jouissance, which, as Lacan says, is useless and does not fit into the Good. In a sense, this chapter shows the reverse of the plot: if the others aim to make psychoanalysis listen to other productions about sexuality than its own, this chapter says something about what those other discourses could learn from the experience of analysis. It is true that, once again, we carry the plague.

The fact that the role of the object exists in eroticism, that is, of the man or the woman on whom *erotic violence*[1] is exerted, poses an irresolvable problem that must be solved. The solution will have to be precarious. It generates, in my perspective, a point of instability insomuch as there is someone who, *as a subject*, occupies the role of an object. When I say *as a subject*, I mean someone who surrenders themself to their own jouissance, and not someone who seeks to sacrificially offer themself to satisfy the supposed jouissance of the Other – much less someone who is, against their will, reduced to the role of an object by another. Embodying the erotic object is a beautiful and dangerous game because, on the horizon, there is always the possibility of being the object of violence, exploitation, rape, and so on. Like many things in life that are really worthwhile, taking on the role of the erotic object is risky.

To clarify what I want to say, I will make use of a conversation that I had by chance. They told me about two young women who were vehemently opposed to a pickup line,[2] considering it a disgusting, sexist act that reduced the place of the woman[3] to that of an object.

The aunts, more experienced in erotic affairs (and/or from another generation), were of a different opinion. They believed that, depending on the way it was delivered, one can enjoy receiving a pickup line. The next day, their nieces sent an email with phrases like "I'll suck you everywhere" and

DOI: 10.4324/9781003252160-7

the comment: "Now do you see that pickup lines are disgusting?" The aunts replied that it was not a pickup line, but a crude remark. I use this example because it seems to me that it presents, in a relatively simple way, all the complexity of the very thorny issue of the role of the object and erotic violence.

"I'll suck you everywhere" – is it a pickup line? It is a question of semantics: to what point do we extend the meaning of a pickup line? Let us start by consulting dictionaries, which are the codification of language. The one from the Royal Spanish Academy defines a pickup line as "short saying with which some quality of someone is pondered, especially the beauty of a woman". According to this definition, "I'll suck you everywhere", is clearly not a pickup line. In those words, there is no pondering of beauty or any other quality, at least not explicitly. The Dictionary of Use of Spanish, by María Moliner, defines a pickup line as "flattery, adulation"; as "praise expressed to a person, said to them", and particularly as a "compliment or flirtatious remark addressed to a woman". According to the Oxford dictionary in Spanish, the pickup line is a "word or expression of admiration, flattery, or praise that is directed towards a person". According to this definition, one word would be enough for a pickup line, which is addressed to a "person" – not necessarily a woman. We would hardly consider "I'll suck you everywhere" as an expression of admiration or flattery, although the person who uttered it may have admired something about the woman to whom it is directed. According to Wikipedia, a pickup line is a "compliment or adjectival phrase that is normally addressed to a woman" and differs from

> the closest synonyms such as courtship, flirting, or crude remark, since it refers to words that are directed to an unknown woman, on the street or in another open and public space, recognizing her beauty and drawing attention in front of others.[4]

In an old conference in Caracas,[5] whose date I cannot specify because it does not appear in the publication (but was surely in the decade of the eighties), Jacques-Alain Miller (drawing on the book "*El humorismo en el español hablado*", by Werner Beinhauer) defines the pickup line in a very interesting way. Miller says that the pickup line supposes:

> that the man delivering the pick up line does not aspire to retain the woman. If there is an erotic message, an erotic connotation, there is at the same time, remarkably, a profound disinterest – a disinterest that makes the pickup line, when it reaches its ultimate form, an aesthetic activity.
>
> (Miller, n.d., 31)

We could hardly consider "I'll suck you everywhere" as an aesthetic activity. Miller places the pickup line at the level of wit, which, as such, implies an infraction. He notes that it is not only an infraction of the code of language, but "the infraction of a pickup line is doubled by the fact that it is also an infraction of the code of decency" (32). However, I will add that, when it achieves what Miller calls "its ultimate form", it is an infraction that can be accepted, sanctioned with a smile, a blush, or a drop of the eyes.[6] The pickup line, continues Miller, following Beinhauer's book, does not make a direct reference to sexual relations (which would leave "I'll suck you everywhere" clearly outside the definition of a pickup line) "on the contrary, it always points a little to the side, at secondary, subaltern elements" (33). However, the pickup line,

> through its highest praise, is also an aggression, a hyperbolic aggression at times; the bombast of its elocution to the woman is also correlative to a dismissal of her condition. That is why it can be framed as an offense, and that is why there is a gray area between the praise and the offense. I think of that pickup line of this compilation in which the man says to the woman "Thief." There we find something that is evidently between insult and praise. We also see it in the pickup lines that only rest on the breaking up the woman's body into separate pieces, where the praise of special parts of her body taken to a symbolic value supposes, effectively, that it is not directed at a person but at the fetishistic value of parts of her body.[45]

"I'll suck you everywhere" falls into the category of a crude remark; it can hardly be heard as flattery or praise. What is interesting is the series "pickup line, courtship, flirting, crude remark" cited in the Wikipedia article, or that "gray area" between praise and offense that Miller cites. If "crude remark" is among the "close synonyms" of a pickup line, if for the nieces it was an example of what they reject in the pickup line, there must be something that connects them as if that crude remark were a kind of failed pickup line. That crude remark, then, has a complex relationship with the pickup line; it is the opposite (the pickup line would be closer to gallantry), but, at the same time, it has something in common, that makes it possible, at the very least, to ask if "I'll suck you everywhere" is either a pickup line or a crude remark.

It does not end up being a pickup line because it is not metaphorical; it did not find (or did not seek) the correct phrasing. However, at the heart of the pickup line, insofar as it addresses the erotic object, veiled by the metaphor, there will always be something on the order of "I'll suck (and here we can replace the verb with others, although not that many) you everywhere". I mean that on the horizon of the pickup line, more or less distant, more or less achievable, or even in an asymptotic relationship with its realization, there will always be the sexual act, in which the dimension of the erotic object appears.[7]

It is a failed pickup line that remains as a crude remark – not because it degrades, but because it *only* degrades. For a subject to be able to occupy the role of the erotic object without losing their dignity as a subject or feeling excessively violated,[8] it is necessary that they must be both valued and degraded, loved and desired. What makes "I'll suck you everywhere" so harsh is that it only takes on one aspect, and makes the drive present without giving it the framework in which it would be tolerable; that is why it is repulsive to those who listen to it. Everything indicates that this role of being the object, this valued/degraded role, even when it is possible to give it a framework that makes it acceptable, generates difficulties (and a lot of attraction too!) both for those who occupy the masculine role of a subject, as well as for those who occupy the feminine role of an object.[9] On the feminine side (and I repeat that I am not talking about genders) we find the difficulty of a subject being an object, while, on the masculine side, that of supporting the subjective division in the form of simultaneously valuing and degrading, loving and exerting violence, protecting and harming. The clinical experience shows that this is one of the greatest difficulties, if not the greatest, of erotic life.[10]

This role of the erotic object also poses a problem for psychoanalysis. It is a difficulty that does not occur randomly: psychoanalysis, as I understand it, is oriented to the promotion of the subject, and seeks to place under question the subject's identification with a certain object in particular, namely, the phallus,[11] that would supposedly complete the desire of the Other. Therefore, in this sense, psychoanalysis leads the subject to give up the position of the object. The point is that being identified with the phallic object of the Other is a narcissistic identification, while the role of the object in the erotic experience is a threat to narcissism. It is making oneself suffer the threat of fragmentation, degradation, or failure to the ideals with which the ego identifies. If the subject identifies with the phallic object, the desire of the Other governs and the desires that threaten the narcissistic identifications are repressed, while, for someone in a feminine position, embodying the role of the object in the erotic scene means bringing one's own jouissance to the limit of fragmentation, loss of dominance, value, and power – all reassuring attributes of narcissism. For this reason, embodying the role of the object can be distressing. If an analysis loosens the phallic-narcissistic identifications of a subject, it is because those identifications prevent them from accessing what is beyond the pleasure principle, that is jouissance, which goes beyond the barriers of narcissism, of Good, of measure.[12] If a psychoanalyst confuses these two meanings of the word object and interprets them as equivalent, they would be working to reinforce narcissism (and neurosis), even if they believe that they are giving place to the subject.

This confusion is not random. There are two candidates who occupy the role of the subject: the ego and the subject of the unconscious. Perhaps it is more accurate to say that the ego tends to believe itself to be the subject, the one who handles the language, the one who decides and needs to believe itself to be, paraphrasing Freud, the master in its own house. It is a necessary illusion, moreover, without which one cannot live. We analysts, who carry our own ego, are not exempt, of course, from letting ourselves be fooled by the same mirage and confusing the subject that we want to summon with the ego that is convinced to dominate the game, when in reality it is nothing more than a pawn in a chess match that the subject is unfamiliar with.

Of course, these positions and jouissances of the erotic scene have enormous ramifications in everyday life; they determine it to a great extent. Being the object in the erotic scene makes it easy to shift to simply being an object – having to shut up, having no rights, being subjected to the will of another, being humiliated, etc. It is enough to keep feminism in mind to perceive all the struggle that was necessary to be able to separate these two meanings of the word "object".

Claiming the right to think, to speak, to decide, to choose, to study, to have access to culture, money, and the free enjoyment of one's own body, necessarily implies assuming the place of a subject. The claim, the demand, and the struggle lead the person who embodies them to speak, to say something (in the strongest sense of the term), and that automatically places us as subjects. The dilemma that arises, as I understand it, is how to be a subject without masculinizing oneself – how to not lose femininity in the midst of the feminine claim. It is the criticism that many times is made of a certain feminism: in its vindication, it runs the risk of being completely on the phallic side, in a specular tension with respect to what it fights.

This is not something that only occurs when the woman occupies the role of the object in heterosexual relationships. The role of the erotic object is not simple in gay male culture either, and the "passive" gay (generally called "the feminine passive" within the community) is subject to the same degradation. After attending a conference on Gay Shame, Leo Bersani[13] comments that "Queer intellectuals are curiously reticent about the sexuality they claim to celebrate" (Bersani, 2008, 31) (here the subject appears divided between celebration and reluctance), and is shocked by the silence about what he considers "a major shame-inflicting weapon" (31): AIDS. What is that silence attributed to? Not only to the defense or strategy against homophobia but to "certain shame-inducing mechanisms internal to the gay community itself". (33) It is a "potential sexual shame" (33) to be a carrier of HIV, insofar as "for the overwhelming majority of HIV-positive gay men, to acknowledge being infected amounts to a sexual confession: I have been fucked". (33) Just like in the straight world, it is *not* shameful confessing to having fucked, but to having been fucked – being that object *that enjoyed* being fucked. Leo Bersani says that while many gay men may freely admit (but generally to other gay men) that they like to be fucked, "a significant number of less liberated brothers may still subscribe, perhaps secretly, to the view that Foucault, in a 1982 interview, attributed to most homosexuals according to which 'being the passive partner in a love relationship' is 'in some way demeaning'". (33) The subtle game that occurs in this quote is very interesting: what can and cannot be said, what the Other (which is clearly not singular) enables as a legitimate discourse or not. Some would continue to feel ashamed to confess that they enjoyed being fucked, but it is also shameful to admit that they feel ashamed because that collides with the new ideals, which do not finish displacing the old ones. This gives us the idea of a shame that resists, that imposes itself even despite the change in ideals. The way I see it, I understand that this shame is inescapable because there is a jouissance in it. A great lesson from the experience of psychoanalysis is that shame, humiliation, and even pain, as feelings of the erotic experience, can be not only endured but also cause jouissance – and I am *not* talking about psychopathology. It is an eroticized shame, related to embodying a role of the object that implies a problem without a solution.[14]

Leo Bersani goes on to say that, while the political creed of the gay men who participated in the conference includes being a feminist,

> they would probably feel uncomfortable publicly investigating, first, homophobic shame associated with being HIV-positive, and, second, the involuntary misogynistic shame of being exposed to others (gay and, even worse, straight) as having succumbed to, or actively sought, the sexual «position traditionally associated with female sexuality».
>
> (33)

That is, in our terms, the position of the object. Everything political is authorized in some idea of the Good, but we, psychoanalysts, will be there to remind (I think that in this matter it is our main contribution, which possibly only we will sustain) that desire and jouissance, which are essential, do not adapt to the Good.

The demands of the democratic game, which cost so much blood to achieve,[15] suppose we all claim ourselves to be subjects of the law, that we respect others and make ourselves respected. It is and must be so. However, there is something in eroticism that will always be a stain on the mural of democracy and the most progressive of policies, something that will never harmoniously adapt to its demands. This is just that in the field of eroticism, one enjoys being the object and one enjoys crossing the barrier of respect. As a friend told me the other day about a guy he liked – By God, I wish he didn't respect me so much!

Notes

1 See Bataille, G. (1962). *Death and sensuality, A study of eroticism and the taboo.* Walker and Company. Bataille considers, and I agree, that there is inherent violence in eroticism.
2 Pickup line attempts to translate the Spanish word "piropo", which is a practice in Spanish-speaking cultures which does not have an equivalent in English-speaking cultures. The chapter's development will make this clearer.

3 The perception of what a pickup line is, like so many other things related to the relations between the sexes, has changed a lot in recent times. There is a tendency to consider it as a form of sexual harassment, precisely to the extent that it would reduce the woman to the position of an "object" and violate her. Certainly, this is accurate in many cases (perhaps most), but I hope it becomes clear in this chapter that I distinguish what is street harassment or a crude remark from what is a pickup line. Anyway, I tried to talk to many women to understand their points of view on the matter and not be swayed by my own prejudices.

The result of my small survey notes, at first glance, a difference between the response from women of my generation (at this moment I am 58 years old) and the younger ones. Without hesitation, those of my generation tell me that they like being the recipient of a pickup line. They even said that, depending on their mood, a vulgar remark can make them laugh or feel amused. In general, the younger women initially responded that they never like pickup lines, but, when one questions more deeply, it is clear that this is not always true. A friend from a generation in between mine and that of the youngest women, expressed very well a response that I find very widespread:

> a well-said pickup line can be received well; it seems to me that if the guy surprises me, says it tactfully, and is cute, then I like it. If this is not the case, it can cause me to reject him.

Where the weight of the heteronorm is clearly noticeable is in that women or gays, although they often have the impulse to deliver pickup lines to a man (according to my small survey), rarely do so; the feeling prevails that it is not allowed, does not correspond, or is embarrassing for them.

4 https://es.wikipedia.org/wiki/Piropo_(social) This "drawing attention in front of others" opens up another dimension to the pickup line – one that is not directed towards the woman but at peers, at other men, seeking a reaffirmation of their masculinity in front of others and from others. However, given the focus of this chapter, it is an avenue that I will not explore.

5 Miller, Jacques-Alain, Cinco conferencias caraqueñas sobre Lacan, Editorial Ateneo de Caracas, Venezuela. Without a print date.

6 Miller takes, from the aforementioned book by Werner Beinhauer, the example of a Sevillian boy whose pickup line consisted of a simple "Oh", "with an accent between soft and deep", and notes that "In its brevity, it feels at the same time as all the deepest meanings of existence are mobilized". Idem, page 40.

7 Some friends who read this writing pointed out something that I had overlooked because I am not a woman: namely, the woman who is presented with the pickup line does not have a choice about hearing the compliment and is forced to do so whether she likes it or not, which in itself already contains a note of violence. Even, for some, the pickup line could only take place when previously consented to. I hear what they have to say, but I am not very convinced that we would live in a better world if everything were previously agreed upon and explicitly consented to.

8 I clarify "excessively" because the ideal of complete non-violence has nothing to do with eroticism. I refer again to Bataille's book.

9 It can be controversial that I associate the masculine with the subject and the feminine with the object (regardless of the genders of those who embody those positions), but I hope the entire chapter makes it clear that I am referring to the role of the erotic object; that is, as I insist on specifying, of someone who, *as a subject*, occupies the role of an object, and by no means that of someone who is reduced to the role of an object by another person.

10 See Freud, Sigmund, On the universal tendency to debasement in the sphere of love, (Freud, 1957 [1910], 177).

11 In psychoanalysis, "phallus" has many meanings. In this context, I am referring to the phallus as the object to which the subject identifies themself to try to fill the lack in the Other.

12 I find the psychoanalytic literature on jouissance extremely confusing. The book that most influenced my way of thinking about it (and which is not confusing!) is the same one that I harshly criticized for its points on sexuality: Lágrimas de lo real, by Norberto Rabinovich, which fittingly, has the subtitle, Un estudio sobre el goce. Furthermore, I feel indebted to Norberto Rabinovich's teachings in his seminars.

13 Leo Bersani (1931) is an American professor, who specialized in French litera-ture. He has moved on from studies focused on French literature to interdisci-plinary research touching on psychoanalysis, lesbian & gay studies, art, queer theory, painting, and film. He is a regular contributor to the psychoanalytic magazine L'Unebévue.

14 If we managed to be so conceited, so progressive that we no longer felt any sexual shame, perhaps the ego would gain dominance, but surely, some of the jouis-sance of the erotic experience would be lost. Fortunately, there is no chance of that happening anyway.

15 Democracy in Argentina, and Latin America in general, is not nor has been easy to sustain, and they have been interrupted by violent and bloody military dictatorships.

Bibliography

Bataille, G. (1962). *Death and sensuality, a study of eroticism and the taboo.* New York, NY: Walker and Company.

Bersani, L., & Phillips, A. (2008). *Intimacies.* Chicago, IL and London: The Univer-sity of Chicago Press.

Freud, S. (1957). *The standard edition of the complete psychological works of Sigmund Freud, Volume XI (1910).* London: The Hogarth Press.

Miller, J. (n.d.). *Cinco conferencias caraqueñas sobre Lacan, Editorial Ateneo de Caracas.*

Moliner, M. (1994). *Diccionario de uso del español.* Madrid: Gredos.

Rabinovich, N. (2007). *Lágrimas de lo real.* Rosario: Homo Sapiens Ediciones.

6   Rethinking the possible as such

To Judith Butler

An English teacher, in a school in the province of Buenos Aires[1] "where there is not always chalk to write on the blackboard; where no bells ring to go out to recess, because there are none" (Ramos, 2014, para. 4) described in an article an experience that moved him: a colleague showed him a piece of paper that he took from some students in class. It said: "My mom wanted a woman, and my dad a man. But the only thing that came out was me – a fag". At the bottom of these verses appears the name of a ten-year-old boy who, three years ago, dared to tell the whole school that he "feels gay, that he likes boys, and not girls in the same way" (Ramos, 2014, para. 2). Of course, it is not possible to know who wrote the verses, if it was the boy himself or his classmates to make fun of him. What is interesting about these verses is that, regardless of whether the child or his classmates wrote them, they accept the fact that not everyone can be placed into the category of a "man" or a "woman". In terms of queer theory, it can be said that they question gender binarism.

This questioning is by no means without repercussions.

> What that little boy faces every day for daring to openly live his desire is terrible. I hear the insults of his classmates when they go out for recess. It is terrible to know, from my own experience, what awaits him.
>
> (Ramos, 2014, para. 5)

Far away from the province of Buenos Aires, in Berkeley, California, Judith Butler wrote in 1999: "I grew up understanding something of the violence of gender norms (...) It was difficult to bring this violence into view precisely because gender was so taken for granted at the same time that it was violently policed" (Butler, 1999, xix). In response to this violence that she knows so well, Judith Butler wrote a book, *Gender Trouble*, that established an inevitable milestone. It is a text whose

> ...dogged effort to "denaturalize" gender....emerges...from a strong desire both to counter the normative violence implied by ideal morphologies

DOI: 10.4324/9781003252160-8

of sex and to uproot the pervasive assumptions about natural or pre-sumptive heterosexuality that are informed by ordinary and academic discourses on sexuality ... It was done from a desire to live, to make life possible, and to rethink the possible as such.

(xx)

The violence of gender norms, which has also been called compulsory het-erosexuality, establishes what Judith Butler labeled "intelligible genders" ("male" and "female") and others that are not. "How must we rethink the ideal morphological constraints upon the human such that those who fail to approximate the norm are not condemned to a death within life?" asks Butler (xx). Hence, the book is "part of the cultural life of a collective strug-gle that has had, and will continue to have, some success in increasing the possibilities for a livable life for those who live, or try to live, on the sexual margins" (Butler, 2007, p. 32) like, for example, our little boy from the prov-ince of Buenos Aires.

Do the theory and practice of psychoanalysis also help improve the life chances of those who do not respond to compulsory heterosexuality or gender binarism? Is psychoanalytic theory part of the violence of gender norms, or is it, rather, on the side of rethinking the possible as such? The first difficulty in answering this question is that there is no *one* psychoanalytic theory. While I was taking notes for this chapter, Silvia Amigo[2] published a book, *La autorización de sexo*, which I find representative of theoretical positions that, concerning this matter, seem very generalized.

Some points from the book draw my attention – especially some omis-sions. I will start with a detail: the image chosen for the cover of the book is that of Adam and Eve, painted by Lucas Cranach the Elder in 1533. Al-though the text, following Lacan, criticizes the "naturalism" of Ernest Jones and his "God created them male and female" stance, the book is preceded by that image so charged with meaning.

As the title indicates, the book will deal with the "authorization of sex", an expression that the author attributes to Lacan. I couldn't find it in Lacan's texts or seminars right through my research; the closest thing I found was in the class of April 9, 1974, of the XXI Seminar, *Les non-dupes errent*, where he says "the sexed being is authorized only by him/herself".[3] Authorizing oneself, according to Silvia Amigo, is restricted to "authorizing oneself as a man or a woman". However, this authorization is not guaranteed: "In re-ality, the twists and turns of personal history do not ensure that a subject will self-authorize as male or female" (Amigo, 2014, 10). We would then have subjects that authorize themselves as male or female and others that do not. As for these "other" subjects, the text completely ignores them; they are left in outer darkness. Could these be the unintelligible lives that Judith But-ler talks about? We are told that subjects who have authorized themselves "inhabit the field of neuroses", insofar as "psychotic individuals, of course, carry out intercourse or any other genital activity (...) in practice but, by right, make no argument for the phallic function". Something very curious for a Lacanian text on sexuality is that throughout the more than 90 pages dealing with the issue of the authorization of sex, from the Lacanian structural triad of neurosis-psychosis-perversion, the perverse structure is never mentioned.[4] Neither the word homosexuality nor any of its synonyms are used even once, and no mention is made of any of the variables of erotic life that do not refer to male-female polarity. If an imaginary extraterrestrial were to have this text as a reference to get an idea of human sexuality, it would believe that on this planet there are heterosexual men and women on one side and, on the other, crazy people who perform intercourse in practice but not by right.

As if it were an irrelevant detail, we are told *en passant*, that "nothing forces a speaking being to inscribe on one side or the other of the graph [of the sexuation formulae]", just to have this immediately contradicted (about "masculine attributes") by the claim that "the fact of destiny ascribed to the anatomy is not without consequences". The fact of destiny being that "man possesses a penile organ (...) and in that organ he will find an obstacle to inscribing himself on the feminine side" (65). Omitting the fact that "man" is once again solely defined by anatomy, Silvia Amigo writes as if she were unaware that there are many men for whom the "penile organ" is not an obstacle to inscribing themselves on the feminine side.

"This does not prevent", the text continues, "that well-endowed men, such as Saint John of the Cross, inscribe themselves on the feminine side, obtaining another kind of jouissance, despite the hindrance that the organ may cause them" (65). I find it all very bizarre: with millions of men who can enjoy taking the role of an object in a sexual relationship through anal intercourse, is it necessary for the only example cited of feminine jouissance in a male to be a mystic and a "well-endowed" male? Is there not a huge part of the reality here that, in a very significant way, is omitted? Precisely that part is pointed out by the boy from the province of Buenos Aires or his classmates, as well as Judith Butler with her theory, the part that challenges that not everything can be encompassed under the naturalized figures of "man" and "woman".

Returning to my question: Is Silvia Amigo's book, considered as an example of a certain type of discourse prevalent in much of Lacanian psychoanalysis, one that is going to contribute to a possible life – an intelligible life – for the child of the province of Buenos Aires? Does it reinforce or challenge "the pervasive assumptions about natural or presumptive heterosexuality?" In my opinion, with its insistence on authorizing oneself as "man" or "woman" being the only "acceptable" option, the book itself is part of the violence of gender norms. I repeat, I am not singling out Silvia Amigo in particular, but her text was one that I came across by chance, and I consider it representative of a very generalized way of thinking.

Judith Butler says,

> The task here is not to celebrate each and every new possibility qua possibility, but to redescribe those possibilities that already exist, but which

exist within cultural domains designated as culturally unintelligible and impossible. (...) Cultural configurations of sex and gender might then proliferate or, rather, their present proliferation might then become articulable within the discourses that establish intelligible cultural life, confounding the very binarism of sex, and exposing its fundamental unnaturalness.

(Butler, 1999, 189)

Rethink the possible as such.

Notes

1 The Buenos Aires Province is the largest and most populous Argentinian province.
2 Silvia Amigo is a well-known Argentine psychoanalyst and psychiatrist of Lacanian orientation.
3 Lacan, Jacques, Seminar XXI, Les non-dupes errent, unpublished. http://www.lacaninireland.com/web/wp-content/uploads/2010/06/Book-21-Les-Non-Dupes-Errent-Part-3.pdf.
4 I would very much agree if it were meant to denounce the contradictions of the concept of perversion, but here it is about something else – a suspicious and downright omission.

Bibliography

Amigo, S. (2014). *La autorización del sexo y otros ensayos*. Buenos Aires: Letra Viva.
Butler, J. (1999). *Gender trouble. Feminism and the subversion of identity*. New York, NY and London: Routledge.
Ramos, T. (2014). http://izquierdadiario.com/Lo-unico-que-salio-fui-yo.

7 Felix Julius Boehm

In the class of May 13, 1959, at the seminar on *Desire and its Interpretation*, Jacques Lacan returns once again to speak on desire and its object, pointing out the novelty that psychoanalysis brings concerning the philosophical conception of the object as an object of knowledge. The object of desire leads him to the formula of fantasy, to castration, and to its object, the phallus. He recognizes that the level of abstraction that he is dealing with can be a bit exhausting, and in order to relax a bit, he says he will illustrate it in terms of concrete experience. He chooses homosexuality.

In the early days of psychoanalysis, he says (and not so much "in the early days", since he references the year of publication of Three Essays, that is, 1905), homosexuals were not analyzed. I do not know what he is referring to, as far as I know, Freud never refused to take a homosexual in analysis. Continuing with his narrative, Lacan affirms that "then we began to analyze homosexuals". Here he, always so sparing in the recommendation of other analysts, begs his audience to refer to "the very exemplary works of Felix Boehm" (Lacan, 2013, 437). Who is this psychoanalyst that Jacques Lacan invites us to read?

Born in Riga in 1881, his father was an industrialist and his mother was the daughter of a merchant. Felix and his two brothers belonged to a group of Baltic Germans connected to Alfred Rosenberg, the main ideologue of National Socialism. After a brief foray into engineering, he studies medicine in Geneva, Freiburg, and Munich. His teachers include Emil Kraepelin and Ernst Cassirer. We do not know how it is that he decides to start a career as a psychoanalyst, but we do know that in Munich he was a patient of Eugénie Sokolnicka, the Polish disciple of Freud. In 1913 he joined the Munich regional group of the International Psychoanalytic Association. In 1919, after having voluntarily served as a doctor in the First World War, he settled in Berlin, where he underwent analysis with Karl Abraham. From 1923 onward for ten years, until its closure by the Nazis, he taught at the Berlin Psychoanalytic Institute. In other words, in the most sophisticated place for training analysts that existed at that time.

While Hitler was rising to power, the psychiatrist Matthias Göring, cousin of Marshal Hermann Göring (Hitler's lieutenant and supreme commander

DOI: 10.4324/9781003252160-9

of the Luftwaffe[1]), initiated the "Aryanization of psychoanalysis" and addressed some non-Jewish analysts willing to set off on the adventure: Felix Boehm and Carl Müller-Braunschweig. They were delighted, not so much because of previous membership in the Nazi party but simply because it allowed them to further their career faster. Max Eitingon, as a Jew, had no choice but to leave the presidency of the German Psychoanalytic Association and Boehm did not miss the opportunity to occupy it. The Boehm-Müller-Braunschweig team, already in control of the situation (except, of course, that Göring had the last word) began the "rescue of psychoanalysis" operation. The idea is that in order not to give the Nazis any pretext for banning psychoanalysis, the best thing to do was ... get ahead of them. Then the few Jewish members who had not yet taken the path of exile were forced to "voluntarily" resign from the German Psychoanalytic Association, which would now be truly German, without "impurities". Ernest Jones, at the time (1935) president of the I.P.A. accepted the policy (for the moment with the endorsement of Freud) and presided over the session in which the expulsion of the Jewish members is put into effect. When the *Deutsche Institut für Psychologische Forschung* [German for Institute for Psychological Research], better known as the Göring Institute, was founded, the German Association for Psychoanalysis was finally absorbed, a euphemism for dissolved. The new institute, purged of any Jewish elements, occupied the building of the Berlin Psychoanalytic Institute, designed by Ernst Freud. Boehm was invited to join the administrative council.

Boehm was always interested in homosexuality, to which he devoted several articles and "investigations" in which the possibility of "curing" it through psychotherapy was explored. Starting in 1939, he led a research team at the Göring Institute that studies homosexuality and launched a case study. He was appointed as an "expert" on homosexuality of the *Wehrmacht*[2], especially the *Luftwaffe*. At first, he limited himself to denouncing the "homosexual danger" that supposedly weighed on Germany, asking the Reich to take surveillance and early diagnostic measures (it seems that he continued with the policy of "anticipating events"), but finally, in 1944 when the war was getting worse and scapegoats were being sought, he accepted the Nazi "program" and sent the homosexuals he cared for or examined as an "expert" to a scheduled death. All the while pretending to save those who suffered from psychosis or alcoholism: a true humanitarian.

Geoffrey Cocks informs us, in his book *Psychotherapy in the Third Reich*, that homosexuality in Nazi Germany was a crime "above and beyond the traditional prohibition of its practice under Section 175 of the German Penal Code" (Cocks, 1985, 206), against which Ulrichs fought, as we saw in Chapter 1.[3] Homosexuals were institutionalized and medicalized "to proscribe degenerates for the protection of the German racial community" (206). For the Nazis, homosexuality was "inconsistent with the manly attributes of the soldierly German Volk, and a deadly peril to the survival of the race. It was regarded as a matter of not just national but biological treason" (206).

Of course, as always, homosexuals were the *others*, along with Jews and Bolsheviks.[4] Despite this, homosexuality was an internal concern within the Nazi party, and Ernst Röhm "certainly was only the most prominent homosexual in the Nazi ranks" (206).

In 1946 John Rickman traveled to Berlin as a representative of the I.P.A. to interrogate Freudians who had served under Nazism, in order to assess their ability to train new candidates. He determined that Boehm was incompetent as a training analyst *not because of his collaboration with Göring and Nazism* but because of his psychic deterioration. It was difficult to reproach him for a policy that at the start had the endorsement of the I.P.A. Nor was his responsibility for the deaths of many homosexuals taken into account.

Felix Julius Boehm died in Berlin in 1958 (the year before the seminary class from which we started), very disappointed, they say, that he had not been re-admitted to the I.P.A.

Would Jacques Lacan know whom he was recommending?

Notes

1 Air Force.
2 Unified armed forces of Nazi Germany.
3 After the war and the domination of the Nazi Party, article 175 of the penal code was not repealed, which prevented many homosexuals from being recognized and compensated as victims of Nazism. They would have to wait until 1969 for it to be repealed for people over 21 years of age and until 1973 for it to be extended to people over 18 years.
4 In the heteronormative order, one could say: "tell me who you consider homosexual and I will tell you who your other/your enemy is".

Bibliography

Cocks, G. (1985). *Psychotherapy in the Third Reich: The Göring Institute.* New York, NY and Oxford: Oxford University Press.
Lacan, J. (2019). *Desire and its interpretation. The seminar of Jacques Lacan Book VI.* Cambridge: Polity Press.

III
Bonus tracks

8 Talking with Jorge Reitter

Neither the Other nor sexuality exists outside of power relations

This conversation, which took place in July 2017, with Manuel Murillo[1] and Pablo Tajman[2] was part of the 'Being an Analyst' cycle, on the blog *Lo que abunda no daña,*[3] which was relaunched and continued on the blog Psychoanalysis and Not Psychoanalysis.[4] The entire first part deals with issues that are independent of the main idea of this book but can be related. First, some of my words on Lacanism will explain why my bibliography is not full of Lacanian texts. Then, there is a fairly extensive discussion on Ferenczi's relationship with Freud. The subject is independent of the main idea of the book (except that Freud would not have hesitated to speak of a "homosexual" relationship, as he did with his relationship with Fliess), but it has something that is related to this book: the difficult decision of daring to speak up. Then, we talk about the topics in this book in a way that I hope makes them especially enjoyable.

Lacan, Lacanism, and the history of psychoanalysis

JORGE: In my opinion, a great damage that Lacan and Lacanism did was erasing the history of psychoanalysis. As if history were Freud, then disaster would come with post-Freudians, nothing to be saved, and then came the enlightened one, or the savior who reminds us of the original truth. A very Christian like story. In my opinion, that is very negative, very negative for thought. Beyond that, Lacan obviously has great qualities, but he also has very terrible ones, really.

PABLO: Furthermore, Lacan has a two dimensional outlook, because at the same time that he is in correspondence with Winnicott and that is the one who has his article *Transitional Objects and Transitional Phenomena* translated into French for the first time, at the same time, by not saying anything, by not removing Winnicott from that group of "post-Freudians" who come to perform the "hecatomb", Winnicott remains included, right? And that produces effects.

J: Sure, there are also remarkable things in the post-Freudians, not only in Winnicott. They were not all stupid until Lacan arrived.

P: Sure, there are a lot of authors.

DOI: 10.4324/9781003252160-11

J: There are even ideas that he takes from the post-Freudians, well, you re-searched it for your book, right?[5]

MANUEL: Yes.

J: But he never acknowledges it, right?

M: It surprised me because, at first, I imagined that I was going to find a ton of philosophers who would talk about this – philosophers and even psychiatrists – but I was surprised by the number of post-Freudians, for example, Jung, Jones, Ferenczi, Winnicott, Klein, Isaacs ... a ton of people who had come up with ideas close to what Lacan later reframed. So, as I went along, I realized that I needed to prepare an important chapter dedicated to post-Freudians.

J: That makes the book much more interesting, in my opinion.

M: When I started, I even gave it the title "What is a post-Freudian?" This is how a chapter of the book begins. It's a question a bit...

J: It's great precisely because it's a way of saying: let's get out of that fixed meaning, transmitted and repeated ad nauseam, right? Well.

P: And that meaning has a lot of power, right? It will even have power in the future because Lacan said it at a certain time in the history of psychoa-nalysis, but it continues to engulf people, the "post-Freudian" category continues to swallow people up, it seems to me.

J: Sure, because it was instituted as the official version within Lacanism. Normally, few people do what Manuel did, going through the trouble to read it and giving a personal opinion.

P: It is true that Winnicott was a bit lucky to not be stigmatized through the years, but there are other authors who did not have such luck, right?

M: Yes.

J: Sure, it's also true that Winnicott or Klein, not to mention, are especially great, but the truth is that there are a lot of people who are remarka-ble, who make contributions. Of course, Lacan is the greatest of the post-Freudians, geniuses do not come along everyday, but that doesn't mean everyone else is disposable... (laughter)

M: Like a unique genius.

The relationship between Ferenczi and Freud

J: Some time ago – let's say a long time ago – I gave a seminar on the relation-ship between Ferenczi and Freud. As I read the articles, and especially the correspondence between the two, my focal point was investigating how Ferenczi arrives at his ideas about the end of analysis, which, in some respects, are so close to those of Lacan. When one comments on what Freud says about the "bedrock", in *Analysis Terminable and Inter-minable*, one overlooks what is nevertheless said in the text -- that Freud is responding to Ferenczi, who had proposed, obviously long before Lacan, that he was trying to go beyond that "bedrock".

Ferenczi has been the object of much ingratitude because neither Winnicott nor Lacan ever acknowledged their debt to him. I gave a seminar on Ferenczi and four or five people came. Nobody thought it was an interesting topic, and yet, the topic was great, *exciting*. Furthermore, the correspondence between them is a novel; it is incredible how Ferenczi finally manages to resolve, against Freud, absolutely against Freud, the transference with Freud, and that is why he comes to his formulations about the end of analysis. And all that did not arouse interest. "Ah, Ferenczi! What could be interesting about him?" they must have thought. "Lacan almost does not name him, *ergo* he does not exist". People ask for Freud/Lacan. And actually: not Freud/Lacan but Lacan, right? Because there is always this idea, so wrong in my eyes, that Lacan is superior to Freud regarding everything. I would not agree with that.[6] In some things, yes. In others, no. Thought isn't so linear, is it?

M: Exactly

J: But what did we want to talk about? (laughter)

P: Let's see if we figure it out... right? (laughter) It seems to me that part of it has to do with our meeting with you...

J: What was it, the video[7] that had come out or that article, where did it come from?

P: No, it was earlier...

M: The article on *Oedipus Gay*,[8] I believe.

P: Afterwards, I looked for some others, Manuel too, we read a bit, then the video came up, and then Cecilia Montenegro told me that you had been at the *Ameghino*,[9] that you had been one of those who introduced other authors.

J: Sure, long before that seminar that I was telling you about, I introduced articles by Ferenczi, as a participant in the Ameghino. At that time, I had been very interested in the issue of the active technique, already seeking greater efficacy in the analyses. And I still believe that he is a great in the history of psychoanalysis. Ferenczi has, in psychoanalysis, the function of the buffoon, he himself said that. The buffoon is the one who tells the truth, but on the condition that no one takes him seriously. Or a Cassandra, who tells the truth but nobody believes her. This is Ferenczi's problem: no one in Freud's environment believed him because no one gave weight to the truth that he was bringing up. Or no one wanted to hear it.

M: Yes, like the *enfant terrible* of psychoanalysis.

J: Exactly. In fact, all the last works of Ferenczi were out of print and sold out for many years. They were not available because the "praetorian guard" was assembled around Freud; a closed circle was assembled to say "this guy is crazy". What was the crazy thing that he said? That the father was castrated. Obviously, like any institution – I would say "religious institution", but I already believe that "institution" and "religious" go together... I don't know if there are non-religious institutions (laughter) – the IPA came out to cover the castration of the father; and the wound that could have opened what Ferenczi raised was immediately healed.

M: Yes, it was like the idea was promoted in the psychoanalytic circles that Ferenczi had not reached the end of the analysis and was still demanding more of the father.

J: Sure. Which, up to a certain point in the relationship between the two was true. It is more complex and that is more insidious, because it is true that Ferenczi demanded a lot of love from him... he was in transference and when one is in transference with someone there is going to be a demand of love, you know? Because it is love and love seeks reciprocity, but he made his mourning and from that mourning came his last formulations, which, I insist, everything Lacan says about the end of the analysis... well, I don't know if everything – I don't know if I know everything – but we can find much of what Lacan says about it in Ferenczi's last papers. And in fact it is said much more kindly and much more honestly.

P: And this idea that the father is castrated? Can you say something else? I have not read much of Ferenczi.

Ferenczi and the end of analysis

J: To start reading, I would recommend above all the correspondence between the two, it is the best document there is. Look, Ferenczi, for me, was the first to realize this: *there is no possibility of ending the analysis if castration is not put into play and, in particular if the analysand does not put into play the castration of the analyst.* It is the castration of the Other, but embodied in the analyst. And that implies doing a certain reading on the analyst's desire, but not to respond to that desire, exactly the other way around: to stop responding to that desire, you have to read it.[10] And what Ferenczi realized is that Freud always rejected any of his ideas that were in that direction. In other words, what Freud did all the time – and very evidently, what I'm telling you is not metaphorical – he told Ferenczi constantly that he wanted him as a soldier of his cause. He called it this: "the cause", it is an expression that Lacan takes when he speaks of "the Freudian cause". He said to Ferenczi: "stop bothering with neurosis, stop bothering with transference, dedicate yourself to psychoanalysis". That, furthermore, was psychoanalysis as Freud understood it.

   When Ferenczi begins to have slightly different ideas, he disagrees on some points with Freud's thinking. Always the ghost, I would almost tell you Freud fears that he is another Jung. (That is another topic that I would be passionate about investigating: what happened in the relationship with Jung, how much of Jung's end with psychoanalysis has to do with the rejection, which Freud also does, of Jung's transfer to him?) So Ferenczi begins to realize this: that if the analyst cannot bear to put his castration into play, it greatly complicates the patient's exit. He begins to realize what he calls the imposture, I think he calls it that: the imposture or professional hypocrisy. He begins to realize very simple things but which are very important. For example, a patient comes and says "hey, you're in a bad mood today". He would say,

Well, that may be a fantasy of the patient, obviously, but you might be in a bad mood. And if you're in a bad mood, the best thing you can do is to tell your patient: 'yes, I'm really in a bad mood'.

Because if not, all the time you are rejecting: first, that he is doing a good read; and second, you are rejecting that you are not always the analyst in function; there are things of your subjectivity, beyond your desire as an analyst, that are going to inevitably sneak in. It even seems to me that it is okay for them to sneak in, that a "perfect" analyst would not be a good analyst.

P: That rejection is maddening, right? Because you are also saying: "your perception is not valid".

J: Exactly. It is properly maddening, but it happens. Things like this happen all the time, analyzes that have this logic: you can put into play the castration of the whole world, obviously of your mom, dad, wife, husband, whoever you want... but not that of the analyst. From that complex situation that Freud's resistance put him in, to falling from his transferential place, Ferenczi manages to go off on a tangent that allows him to resolve it. If he had been locked into the transference with Freud... and, notice that I say "the transference with Freud", I do not say the "analysis", because although Freud had him in the consulting room for three periods, he always had him reluctantly, he did not want to analyze him. Ferenczi tried to force Freud to analyze him, but it was not indifferent that Freud did not want to, obviously. *Ferenczi gradually discovers that the problem is the analyst's narcissism. It is always narcissism that rejects castration.*

Ferenczi, in order to resolve his transfer with Freud, made a kind of tangent with Groddeck. You know Groddeck, the one who invented the concept of the *Id*? Well, Ferenczi gets along very well with Groddeck, they have a great empathy. Talking with Groddeck he begins to analyze his transference with Freud but, obviously, that seems to me a great lesson as an analyst, you always need Other. If the Other, (which for Ferenczi was Freud) does not give rise to your subjectivity to the extent that he feels threatened, you cannot resolve the transference unless you find another Other,[11] as it was in this case Groddeck, who begins to allow it ... in fact, the only testimony we have... I don't know if you know the famous Palermo episode.

P: No...

J: Freud's relationship with Ferenczi starts with a kind of honeymoon that lasted two or three years. I don't remember, I'm very bad with dates, but it lasts a few years until they take a trip together to Italy. It is the trip where Freud writes, or rather, begins to draft Schreber's text – there you have such an interesting framework – because Freud tells, I think Jung, but surely he also told Ferenczi, that everything he learned from paranoia he actually learned from Fliess – now he applies it to Schreber, but he had learned it from Fliess. Not from a Fliess teaching, but from the relationship with him. And Freud commented to Ferenczi, on that trip to Italy, that he was working on his transfer with Fliess at that time.[12] In other words, Freud was elaborating his own "end of analysis" on that trip. When they return from Italy, Ferenczi fears that the relationship has ended, which it doesn't, but something *significant* did happen in the coexistence of both. There is a letter to Groddeck where Ferenczi says (I say it in my words, it is more interesting to read it) something like: "what happened in Palermo is that when we started working together, Freud dictated what I had to write". Then Ferenczi said: "Well, I want to give my opinion too". And Freud said: "Well, do you want to be right about everything?!" Freud led him to that place of being the scribe of his word, and Ferenczi resisted *that*. To a certain extent, what came later in the relationship between Ferenczi and Freud was to elaborate what was revealed there, in Palermo... I don't know if you all have read that famous interview with Freud? A journalist has the *very* clever idea of asking him: "How are you as an analyst?" Do you know that interview? It is brilliant. The guy is brilliant, he doesn't take it for granted and Freud, who, of course, was extremely intelligent and honest, tells the truth: "*As an analyst, I'm not very good because I'm too much of a father*". Let's say, it is Ferenczi's huge effort which allows him to overthrow that *too much of a father*, and the reaction of the *IPA* was declaring him "crazy" in order to silence the truth, to annul it and say "No, the father must not be questioned, Ferenczi is crazy". When Ferenczi reads his famous last work, which for me is, above all, a work on transference –although it is not explicitly stated that way – which is a *Confusion of tongues*, which surely you read or heard of it, he read it in the last congress in which he participates and all the gathered analysts listen to him like this: "Let's be respectful to this old man, who is kind of gaga", but basically no one listens to him, they let him talk like if he were crazy. When he goes to that conference, he reads the work to Freud...

P: Before presenting it?

J: Before presenting it. The conference was in Wiesbaden, in Germany, but since Budapest is very close to Vienna, Ferenczi passes through Vienna, he reads it to Freud and then he went on to the Congress. When he listens to him, Freud asks him *not* to read it, not to read the paper. That is one of the points where I read that –for me–, already at that point he had resolved the transference with Freud, because at another time, Ferenczi would have been devastated by Freud's request and would not have read it. And he, nevertheless, reads it. In other words, that is all an act of speaking up, because when Ferenczi is going to say goodbye – it is the last time they see each other in person – Freud does not shake his hand, that is, he rejects him, he turns his back on him. That was their farewell in person, afterwards they exchanged some more letters. The last letter Ferenczi wrote – who I think died in '33, I'm not sure – he writes that the Nazis are dangerous, that he has to leave Vienna and Freud tells him: "Well, you exaggerate everything, it is not that bad. We are going to have this under control". Ferenczi's destiny: always saying the truth and getting rejected.

M: Did you find the correspondence between Ferenczi and Groddeck? I looked in many places and could not find it.

J: I found it in French. I found it on Amazon and a great friend brought it to me when she traveled to France. Anyway, I'm telling you, passages that are this "great" are few, but they are amazing.

M: Because I have read *The Book of the It* by Groddeck and I find it to be another fascinating character.

J: It's super interesting.

M: Those two together and with the experience of the mutual analysis they had …

Ferenczi's boldness

J: Look, he is someone who dared… Ferenczi was bold. He is criticized a lot, but for me you have to understand his logic. He dared to attempt mutual analysis, to later say "it doesn't work". But he tried different options, not sticking to the same setting *all the time*. He was someone who was *very* concerned, as I am, with the effectiveness of the analysis. It is not just a matter of coming up with ideas, it is about changing something. If not, if something in the discourse does not touch on something real… it is fun, it is cute, interesting, fascinating, etc., but… it seems to me that the point is to touch on something real. Ferenczi had the courage to experiment and then he realized those elementary things – that one needs to realize. There is this patient's request[13] for mutual analysis that he accepts, but, in my opinion, *he accepts mutual analysis because he realizes that somehow, the analyst has to put his castration into play.*

Later, he discovers something absolutely valid when he says: "Well, she has the right to choose who to be analyzed by, but I *also* have the right to choose", that is, "I do not have to put my transfer into play with someone other than the one who I choose as an analyst". Excellent conclusion. There he realizes that mutual analysis is not conducive, but I appreciated much more the courage of having tried it than the opinion of those who look down on him saying "Look at the crazy things this guy does!"…

M: This crazy guy… (laughs)

P: Something to go close to the limits and say "well, I went overboard" but something, that *at this point*, we can expand…

J: Exactly. Moreover, he said: "I know I'm going way too damn far, but then I know how to come back" – he said it more elegantly (laughs) – that is, I like to see what the limit is and then I know how to turn around.

Efficacy in psychoanalysis: can neurosis be resolved?

M: You were talking about efficiency, Jorge, as a topic that interested or worried you. I ask you because there is a lot of talk about the effectiveness of psychoanalysis, what do you think?

J: What do I understand by effectiveness?

M: Yes.

J: That something in the life of the person who comes to be analyzed changes, and that it changes for the better. For them to live, enjoy life more, not waste time, not postpone, be as creative as they can be, have the life they want to have... well... "the life they want to have", I want to be a millionaire, for example (laughs), but the closest thing to the life they want to have. May they enjoy what they have instead of regretting what they lack. To not stop doing the things they can do, not live scared, and solve the neurosis.

Neurosis has two meanings: there is that famous tripartition of the world, according to which everyone should fit into three structures... I don't care too much for this tripartition. When I say neurosis, I mean: *to resolve the position in life of being all the time blocking the castration of the Other, at the cost of one's own desire. That can be solved.* This idea of "neurosis as a structure" is so ingrained that people believe that neurosis has no resolution. I think they are referring to this: it has no resolution in the sense that there will always be the unconscious, there will always be anxiety, I think there will always be guilt – I do not think that all guilt is neurotic, that is a topic that interests me – but that neurosis can be solved isn't a question to me, I know: *it can be solved.* Now, it's not that afterwards life is easy. *It is simply that the problems of life are just the problems of life; It is not trying to make the Other – whatever form it takes – be complete and unquestioned.*

This has everything to do with this search by Ferenczi that I was telling you about. The goal of analysis is not for the analyst to remain intact. If that happens the analysis will never end. When I talk to students, I tell them about the end of the analysis, and I tell them that in addition to the moment it ends, it is what guides the analysis. *There is a very common tendency to believe that they will be analyzed for life.* Almost like they don't want to finish it (I don't know if it's a training topic or another neurosis topic) or maybe, this is our version of the "afterlife": in another life I will finish the analysis. But we could say that there is an afterlife, achievable in this life: beyond the illusion of the Other's completeness, for sure.

An analysis, does it have objectives, purposes?

P: That opens up a topic that interests me a lot and that seems to come up in conversations with young colleagues: the idea of whether or not an analysis has objectives.

J: I listen to the reason each person comes in, I don't force an analysis because not everyone who comes to an analyst's office wants to analyze themselves. But when someone wants to be analyzed, which, I insist, does not always happen, but that it does happen is not independent of what one wants – one: the analyst – that is, it is an encounter between the one who comes and what the analyst offers. When that happens, in my opinion, the objectives that I set for myself are these: to resolve the neurosis (this is how it could be summarized). Enjoy life, do not spend your whole life postponing enjoyment for the hereafter, for some day, no one knows when; and lose the fear of acts. *That for me is the aim of the analysis, to lose the fear of acts. First of all, one has to lose the fear of the act of speaking.* That is why free association is and will continue to be the fundamental rule of psychoanalysis. That little act that we ask the analysand in each session: to speak. For example, since we're going down that road, when Ferenczi, *despite Freud's* request, (*Freud's!* I mean, imagine what Freud meant in 1932), doesn't shut up... that is an act, which for me shows that he came out or is coming out, clearly, in a very strong way, from the neurosis. Because his analyst (who is no less than Freud, *the father* of psychoanalysis) asks him to shut up and he doesn't. He neither shuts up, nor breaks from psychoanalysis (like Jung), and how right he was because regardless of what happened at that time, he *found* his readers. It took some time, but he found his readers. Did you see that quote by Freud? I think it is in *The Future of an Illusion*, which says: "the truth speaks softly, but it insists and in the end it makes itself heard". I do not know if you are aware, but lately in many parts of the world there is a revaluation of Ferenczi's work. Not always from perspectives that interest me the most, but well, of course, each one has their own reading.

The duration of analyses

M: You were saying that neurosis can be resolved and I was wondering: how long would it take?

J: A long time.

M: It is a question I ask you because the historical mismatch amazes me: in Freud's time, one would be analyzed for a few months or at most a year from Monday to Saturday, and in our time one is analyzed once a week, that is the standard. It may vary, there may be variations, but one is analyzed years, even dozens of years.

J: I have asked myself many times and it is great that you point it out, of course. The analyzes were six times a week, I don't know what that experience is like. I don't know if I could take it, I don't know if it has to do with our new times. "I don't know if I could take it": I mean as an analyst or as an analysand. I'm not even sure that it necessarily shortens the analysis, I'm not even sure that that's better, but that it's different, that's for sure.

Normally, the analyses take a long time because one takes a long time – "one" I mean anyone – takes a long time to *complete the mourning processes that involve an analysis*. It is the mourning of what? That there will be a non-castrated Other, the mourning that one is going to respond to what the Other expects, which is totally linked to the previous one, the mourning that things are going to fit in (for example, that there is going to be what in the Lacanian milieu we call *relation between the sexes*), the mourning of accepting that one does not always want what is right. All those mourning processes take time. One understands this process in two college classes, but to embody them... oh my! No?

P: I even thought, going off what Manuel just said, which has always caught my attention and that, surely, it is not something that can be *done*, because even if the experience would be done six times a week, in this time it would be something else.

J: And also, who can pay for it? (laughs)

P: Without a doubt... but suppose that the "Sigmund Freud Foundation" paid us for the research... I am very interested in the idea of the borderline in psychoanalysis, in working with madness, as Winnicott points out that there may be an analysis in complete collusion, where the supposed transference neurosis is analyzed and something really crazy is left out. I wondered if it is not that this way of analyzing is close to "an inpatient", in the sense that all the time you are "refinding" the analyst. Didn't the borderline "encapsulate" a little, didn't he leave, didn't he fix in the setting – in Bleger's terms – something really crazy that later appeared in the work of other authors?

J: But, I don't understand in what way? You say something really crazy was encapsulated, why in those six sessions?

P: No, I am not saying that it is necessarily true, but I ask myself if the device, taken in that way, does not impede issues arising.

J: Hey, you just reminded me of something, I don't know if this exactly answers your question but it has to do with it, and it also helps me clarify a bit more why I am refreshing my mind on what I had worked on about Ferenczi. It is as if Ferenczi were saying this (and I am convinced by my personal experience that this is so): *in a moment, the analysand begins to analyze the analyst*. And, among other things that Ferenczi analyzed about Freud and was right, there are many texts[14] – did you see that everything related to Freud is hyper-documented? – that prove Freud was very bothered by everything that was crazy. He could not stand the madness, he did not stand – not to mention – what he called "perverse". In other words, he could not stand all that (and the very high price that his daughter paid for all that, on the other hand); perhaps something of Freud's desire or limitations has made that madness be excluded.

No analyst hears everything

Another thing that occurred to me from my own experience of the end of the analysis that later I related with what Ferenczi posited and with what some friends told me about their own ending of analysis, is that *no analyst hears everything. There is always a part of the analysis that the analysand does for them, that they have no choice but to do for themselves. If they believe that they are going to go through the whole process in transference, the analysis is going to last forever.* The subjective process that is an analysis has a very important milestone in the fall of the transference. But it does not end there, it enters the last stage of the analysis, in which each analysand has to elaborate on the experience that was the analysis in transference. At this stage, they have to resolve what, inevitably, could not be resolved in the analysis. Everything would be resolved if the analyst was someone who had the capacity to hear everything, which does not happen. So, *there is a part of the analysis that is with the analyst, another that is always against the analyst, and another without the analyst.* At least that is my interpretation of what happened at the end of my analysis, and of what some friends told me about their own experiences, since in general we do not find out what happens after the end of the sessions to our analysands. I remember having learned from an article by Octave Mannoni[15] – which was very good – that there is no self-analysis, that analysis is in transference, which I agree with, but, at the same time, I would say, *there is always self-analysis, there is always a part of self-analysis in the process of analysis.* Although, as I said about Ferenczi, it is never without Other. I'll go even further, I believe that *there is a moment during the analysis – that depends on each analysand – in which the analysand begins to take charge of the analysis and there the end is near.* Another sign that the analysis is heading towards an end, which Ferenczi points out frequently in these last works, is when the analysand overcomes the fear of criticizing their analyst. The analysand has great difficulty in criticizing the analyst, to the point that sometimes it doesn't even cross their mind, then they think about these criticisms and it is likely that they do not even dare to name them. Although, it is true when Freud says that it is much more difficult to say something to someone who is present, than to speak about a third party who is absent. So... well, I got lost (laughs).

Analysis as "mourning", the word as act

M: It surprised me, I found it interesting, that you were talking about the duration of the analysis in the perspective of what leads us to do those mournings.

J: Well what happens is that, *to a large extent, the analysis is a long mourning, it is like a mourning as less traumatic as possible. It is the mourning of the non-existence of the Other or it is the mourning to accept that one does not want only the Good.* They are all ways of saying the same thing. Or it can be said that it is the mourning that one wants, but also does not want to be only the phallus of the Other, then, all that mourning takes a long time. It is a great mourning process that is linked, as I understand it, to give room to desire and that is closely linked to giving room to the word. I would also say that analysis is the process of losing the fear of speaking, but insofar as speaking is an act and not pure blah, because it can also be said that it is the process of losing the fear of acts. What happens is that the act, in the context of analysis, is generally the act of speaking. Obviously, there is an abyss between naming something or not naming it, it is something that interests me a lot. To name or not to name, I think any analyst is sensitive to the *giant* difference between naming and not naming.

P: Listening to you, I was thinking when I first came across the book, now I forgot the author's name, *How to do things with words.* It is the source of the idea of performativity.

M: John Austin

P: There it is, John Austin. Those conferences are after Freud. Reading them – they have a quite accessible style – made me think about what I really like from Lacan, not only what he produced, but also the joints that he left us.[16] For example, the idea that makes some sense, as psychoanalysts, to take something from linguistics, but, one can take what Lacan took or one can change it for something else. And if you take Saussure out a bit and put Austin in, a version of psychoanalysis remains, to my liking, much closer to what we are talking about.

J: Oh, wonderful! What you are saying is great, you take the spirit of what Lacan transmits but do not copy it word for word.

P: Exactly. Authors such as Hugo Bleichmar, who without saying he takes this joint from Lacan (perhaps fights with him a lot because he loved him too much) he does so with Chomsky and generates an idea of psychoanalysis that is very interesting (to my liking) and that takes the idea that it is not without the motivation of the patient and that, therefore, it is not to analyze everything but to analyze in relation to that motivation (or its lack of) and there is another idea of floating attention.

J: Well, I agree with that idea. I think that, maybe I'm exaggerating, but without that attitude psychoanalysis is going to die. It is going to die or subsist as a religion if we don't start playing and seeing the infinite possibilities that exist. As Foucault used to say, something that he repeated in those interviews with him in last years, a phrase that I love - I must not be quoting it literally -: that philosophy was to be able to think that *this can also be thought in another way.* I love the phrase and I love the adverb, this can *also* be thought of in another way. It means that it is not that it is badly thought out, but you can also think in another way, and that other way will open up to other possibilities.

Foucault: identity, psychoanalysis, sexuality

P: It reminds me of an idea by Derrida, which I found reading Ricardo Ro-dulfo,[17] who talks about "non-oppositional differences", that something can differ without opposing. It is very interesting, because we are very used to the binary, something defined by everything that it is not.

J: Sure, one tends to "it's this one" and if not "it's that one". What we say is a little more distressing. It puts more into play that knowing is always conjectural. If you want to get hold of an accurate knowledge, that way of thinking is not going, because it puts into play that all knowledge is that: a reading. Be careful, I do not want to say that this reading has no relation to reality, because a "scientific" discourse, let's call it like this: the "clinical discourse", I want it to capture the reality of the clinic and I do not think that anything can capture the reality of the clinic. But I am also not naive to believe that clinical reality is something that can truly be grasped. Because it is something so extremely complex and so subject to interpretation and so subject to values, to a conception of life that, obviously, is highly conjectural.

P: And it leaves us, as analysts, when we try to keep ourselves in that position, closer to disarming ourselves. To disarm ourselves as people, because there is something about identity that, thought from here, is more provisional...

J: Identity, I think Foucault would have said – and with good reason – is strategic. In other words, at this juncture I am this one, but at another juncture... I am, or I want to be, or my strategy leads me to another identity. Proust was also very sensitive to this lability of identity.

M: Jorge, in your reading or research, what are your thoughts on the Foucault-psychoanalysis relationship? I ask you because sometimes I see that: either Foucault is not read, or Foucault is a "friend" of psychoanalysis, or Foucault has very controversial points... there are several perspectives. It is a very complex and unique relationship.

J: It is a tremendously interesting relationship. Foucault opened my mind. In recent years, I don't think anyone has opened my mind as much as Foucault. Obviously, he wrote that book called *The Will to Knowledge*, the first volume of *The History of Sexuality*, which is an *end-to-end* book written in dialogue with psychoanalysis.

M: And it's what we least read...

J: It isn't read much by psychoanalysts. It is a book which seems relatively easy to read, it is not Lacan, but it is one of those books that seems easy, but is very difficult to understand where it is going. Now: when you understand a little better where he is going... my mind changed radically and I believe I think better thanks to him. I don't think he should be taken, at all, as a kind of enemy of psychoanalysis, nor as a psychoanalyst. He is a philosopher who introduces among other things a genealogy of psychoanalysis and its relationship with power. But what I most want to highlight now is that he introduces what is so important and so unknown in psychoanalysis, which is *the political dimension of sexuality*, how sexuality is completely embedded in power relations. The effect that Foucault had on me reminds me of when Freud says that he did not take into account the death drive before 1920, but once he started thinking like that, he couldn't think otherwise. Same thing happened to me. Before, due to my training as an analyst, I did not take into account that political dimension of sexuality, and once I began to see it, I cannot think otherwise. Well, I don't know if that answers your question.

M: Yes, I was surprised to read in your writing, that you end up saying that psychoanalysis talks about sexuality, being a concept, a notion, whose genealogy it *ignores*.

J: Exactly! Yes. If I said that: I agree! It was correct. Yes, absolutely, I agree with Reitter (laughs)

M: We should interview Reitter, would you join us? (laughs)

J: Sure, *history is castrating*. I could have been a historian. I was not a historian because... being a psychoanalyst is also being a bit of a historian, it is a mixture of historian and ethnologist... because I also like ethnology, field work. I like the contact with living matter, although I like to read a lot too. But I like what happens in the analysis as well, how desire, love, hatred are put into play there. But history, as a discipline, is extremely castrating. Did you see, for example, what happened to you with Lacan's concepts? If you don't do the research, it seems that Lacan is there and everything came out of his mind, like Athena out of Zeus's head, *but when you start to investigate you realize that everything is human, too human,* and in the end more complex. Without of course taking away the genius from Lacan or any other creator, but the process is much more complex. Foucault shows that thinking in terms of sexuality is not obvious. It is not obvious *whatsoever*, in fact humanity thinks in terms of sexuality very recently[18] and the genealogy of that concept, sexuality – this is perhaps the most important thing and where psychoanalysis is most entrapped, in my opinion – is closely intertwined with the genealogy of *normalization dispositifs. The concept of sexuality is indiscernible from the normalization dispositifs in which this concept is forged.* And psychoanalysis, in my opinion and that of some others, was somewhat trapped there.

Is the object the only contingent of the drive? Toward a world where meaning is not assured

Psychoanalysis, regarding eroticism is... I don't know, revolutionary, let's say? ... Freud puts into play ideas that did not exist until that moment. Basically, *one* idea,[19] but the effect it has is *tremendous*: that it is the contingency of the object. And... strangely, Freud does not say, what I would also say, that it is: *the contingency of the aim of the drive.* One could deduce it, but

Freud writes that the object is contingent, he does not clearly say that the aim is *also* contingent.

M: Why do you think that?
J: Because *not everyone desires copulation as the aim of sexuality*, that is, it is not necessary for a human being, man or woman, as a human being, and being sexed, to have sexual intercourse as an aim. Not everyone seeks sexual jouissance through it, it is not necessary.

17 In the heat of the conversation I forgot at least one other idea that is original to Freud and tremendously powerful in its consequences: that of the structurally incestuous character of infantile sexuality and its importance in adult sexuality. (Jorge)

Psychoanalysis launches this idea that is tremendous in its potentiality, an idea that is, one more brick in the task of building a non-religious world, *a truly secular world*, a world where meaning is not assured, a world where the version of a God guarantor of meaning is not the one that governs. However, precisely because it does not think about the political dimension of sexuality, it is trapped in: *the dispositif of sexuality*, which is a highly complex, heterogeneous mechanism that regulates sexuality at all times. Psychoanalysis brilliantly develops (and what it says is incredibly interesting) how the forms of jouissance and identifications that will prevail in this subject throughout his life are gestated in childhood. What Foucault allows (him and all his enormous descendants, all the thought that arises from his investigations, which is impressively fertile as a field of research, having provoked such dissimilar and interesting thoughts) is to frame "sexuality" in its political dimension. Child-father-mother are not closed cells, they live in a world where there is everything: social classes, relationships with institutions, written and customary laws, mass media, and representations of sexuality that are different in each culture... This huge regulation device is present all the time. *It is not something that happens in childhood, it is something that happens all the time.* It happens to the parents too. Sometimes it seems to me that psychoanalysis makes parents seem as if they were sovereign entities, and they are not. Parents are embedded in a structure that determines them in countless ways: economically, politically, representationally, and judicially. Parents as sovereign entities are the child's vision, it is not real. There is another thing that I learned from Foucault: *politics generates subjects, the Other does not exist outside of power relations.* The Other is already immersed in power dynamics from the beginning. *And that is not a detail.* I believe that it is not noticeable in certain conditions, in other conditions it is very important to take it into account. As far as I can imagine, when patients are in a power relationship quite similar to that of their analysts (which is the most frequent situation, because in general, at least in private practice, patients and analysts belong to the middle class) the strength of power relations to determine subjectivity is not very noticeable there. It begins to be noticed more when the analysand, for example, does not have... when his way of living sexuality does not respond to the heteronorm, or when, for example, they belong to another social class. There you begin to notice much more what is at play... sorry, *you could notice much more, because if you don't see it, you don't see it.* And there you run a great risk, it is something that happens all the time, which is what I call *psychologizing.* Not seeing that a part of the way in which this subject presents themself, produces a symptom, does not respond only to their personal history, their oedipal history, or his own fears, anxieties, or guilt, is not explained only by psychic mechanisms, but also responds to an apparatus that is much bigger than that subject, or his family, but that affects them all the time. You all were working,[20] I do not know if in these terms... but for some reason trans people did not approach the Ameghino, because if you told me that it was *one* trans person, or *four*, we would say that it is an isolated problem; Now, if you are saying that *all* trans people do not go to the Ameghino, you are saying that this is not an individual issue, it is not a problem that can only be thought of in terms of *psychology.*

Social struggles and their advances, new starting points in analyzes

P: What you say makes me think... because the relationship between politics and psychoanalysis appears, which is always so complex and interesting. And I had been thinking about the difference in treatment requirements between two homosexual male patients. One comes and tells me "I'm coming for this, for that and also I'm fighting a lot with my boyfriend...". That is a start.

Another patient comes in, never talks about his sexuality and I am struck by the reiteration of the omission. I realize it's a touchy subject and I try to be most... well, to find some nice ways for him to say something about it. Eventually, he tells me that he is *telling himself* for the first time about his orientation and that he was trying very, very hard to not tell himself.

In the first example, when he says to me "well, I am coming because I am fighting a lot with my boyfriend", there is the whole question of social struggles and questions of power that is already settled in a certain way, because he is also telling me: "well, let's start from the idea that I can have a partner" ... there are a lot of things there, the story went on many years. With the other patient, on the other hand ...

J: He couldn't accept himself yet. If the first one went and made that point to you, it is because there is a whole world of previous struggles that allows him to arrive and say that easily and without fear that you will treat him with electro-shock therapy for having said that (laughs), for example, something that not so long ago, was not unthinkable to occur.

P: And in this second example, that of the patient who struggled against his orientation, I clearly felt that at one point he asked me without asking me... he gave me the possibility to judge him, and that I had to explain my position to him regarding sexuality. They are different worlds.

J: And what did you do?

P: And, I tried to tell him what I thought, I was as honest as I could be.

J: Did you explain your position to him?

P: Yes, I told him that it seemed to me that it was one orientation among others.

J: What you did, in my opinion, was enable him so that he could talk about it, that he could talk about it not as pathology. That is an interesting move. Because regarding this *dispositif* of sexuality, you cannot be on the sidelines. In other words, what you did was remove yourself from that intervention of the heterosexuality *dispositif*, because *if you don't make that explicit, the dispositif governs*. Be careful, although in 2017 this is present, luckily... No! What am I saying luckily? By the struggle of many people! ... that is quite worn down but it is still valid. And it also depends a lot – and here also come the power dynamics with all that they imply - it depends a lot on where you come from, if these *dispositifs* are going to be more eroded or less. It is not the same to speak of Buenos Aires or certain neighborhoods of Buenos Aires than a town in the other provinces of Argentina. In a town in those other provinces, things are very difficult for people who do not respond to heteronormative sexuality. And historical times were, as you said with these two patients... a good example...

P: They are contemporaries.

J: They are contemporaries and not. Because at the same time if you... in a paper that I am writing now, I put the example of a gay kid from a small town in La Pampa... it is much more difficult to be gay in a small town. It takes more courage, but that courage is also enabled, it is not just an individual question, it is enabled, because luckily for this kid, he lives in a world where there is internet and where he can form a community, not restricted to such a small place.

P: You made me think you were saying that abstinence does not mean to keep quiet, I had to make my clinical position explicit.[21]

J: I believe that to be true.

P: Because if not... I had not thought about it, you said it clearly, if not what operates is the standard, it is the heteronorm.

Heteronormativity and psychoanalysis

J: That is a very important and basic concept. What governs is the heteronorm. There is no heterosexual *coming out*. Someone *coming out* is always *gay* or lesbian or *trans*. Why? Because what is supposed, what is naturalized is heterosexuality. We will live in a really different world – if this happens, we have no guarantee – when someone you don't know says "I'm in a relationship" you ask them: "with a man, with a woman, with someone non-binary?" Because if not, meanwhile, the natural thing is that if you are in a relationship it is with someone of the "opposite" sex. Precisely, this discovery that Freud makes, this theorization where he says that "there is no pre-established object of the drive", would imply that one can ask that question without offending anyone.

For example, some time ago some friends told me about a clinic where three of the analysts who worked there were gay, but none of the them talked about it. There were, let's say, three analysts in the closet, which as so often was a glass closet. Now, if *one* did not talk about it, we would say, again, that it is an individual problem of that subject. But if the three do not talk about it, it is telling you that there is something up in the institution. I believe that the psychoanalytic institution is very heteronormative. Very. That is why I discuss it in those articles that you read, because there is a very strong heteronormative bias in psychoanalysis.

M: I am very struck by the fact that you make an important nuance between what would be *a heteronormative theory* or what would be *a heteronormative bias*.

J: Sure, I'm not saying that some concepts of psychoanalysis cannot be re-thought to expunge that heteronormativity. It exists and is very strong. And I would tell you that in some respects it is stronger in Lacan than in Freud, even contrary to what people in general think. Lacan is in some respects heteronormative, according to others he is not. When he, for example, is so opposed to any idea of genital harmony, or when he raises his famous aphorism that there is no relation between the sexes, that really goes to the side of de-constructing... but it seems to be, as it has been happening up until now in the history of psychoanalysis: when the theme of Oedipus appears, linked in Lacan to the theme of kinship (Levy-Strauss),[22] or even later in Lacan the theme of sexuation, everything is framed in the male-female binary. And furthermore, when he talks about the famous sexuation formulae, Lacan no longer talks about homosexuality, so we don't really know what he thinks. Practically at that point he doesn't say anything. He says, at some point, something like "this place can be occupied by someone of any anatomical sexuality", but since he does not develop it, like so many things that he tends not to develop, we do not know, it is not very useful.

P: Reading, there was another article that is not *Gay Oedipus*, nor is it the one about psychoanalytic heteronormativity, where you develop that Oedipus is like the police, a certain version of Oedipus like the police who come to straighten polymorphic infantile sexuality. And it made me think, listening to what we talked about: the great difference between the concepts of polymorphic infantile sexuality and constitutional bisexuality. Because one goes from development, with enormous potential, towards taking a certain form; and the other supposes a form that, well... in any case you can say "they're both there", but it is already formatted....

Understanding so as not to demonize normalizing devices

J: Sure, the idea of bisexuality is that it is one thing and the other, that idea that you bring is good. Anyway, I'm going to tell you one thing: *I don't think normalizing dispositifs should be demonized.* Let's say: *just as there is no pre-established object for the drive, obviously you have to offer it an object.* Did you see those people who believe that if they do not give their son or daughter neither a boy or girl name, nor give them boy or girl toys, the son or daughter will find their *true* desire and their *true* identity? *There is no true desire or identity outside of what the Other offers.* That doesn't exist. It is one of the great teachings that psychoanalysts can contribute: there is no subject without the Other.

That Oedipus is an apparatus that tends to heterosexualize, in my opinion, does not even seem wrong in itself. The problem arises when all the subjects do not respond to that. What do we do when the subject does not respond to that? Do you force them to conform to the norm or do you try to listen? It is a bit similar to what I was saying before: not every patient comes to be analyzed, one offers an analysis but if they do not come to be analyzed, what? Are you going to force them? No. Besides, *you can't force them.* You offer something. If a subject comes with a penis, they are offered a masculine place; if they come with a vagina, they are offered a feminine place.[23] But *they are offered something.* Then you have to see what happens and there, it seems to me, the point is posed... it is not like one could leave out the normalizing devices.[24] The issue is what do you do when something does not respond to that: do you force it? Are we going to do it by force or are we going to accept that it is like that? The subject, in principle, will never respond absolutely to the demand or to the cultural demands.

A journey: Beyond oedipal sexuality – when the transference is in line with the heteronorm helping to perceive power relations – building community with others with the help of the internet.

M: You mark at that point an important difference between the constitutive and something of later life... as if they were two different times to consider.

J: Psychoanalysis has great theoretical developments on infant sexuality and the oedipal phase. But, sometimes, it seems that we talk as if the construction of sexuality ended there. What is also true for certain aspects of sexuality, in childhood the foundations of certain circuits of jouissance and of certain identifications that persist throughout life are established. But sexuality is not limited to that, it is something more complex that is being constituted and, above all, is being *regulated* all

the time. For someone who, for example, is gay, it is tremendously important what begins to happen the moment adolescent sexuality ex-
plodes, when sexuality is no longer infantile sexuality. What happens
at that moment at the relational level, that is, the inevitable clash with
the heteronorm, will also leave indelible marks. And if as analysts we do
not understand a little better what is happening there, it is very likely,
almost certainly, that in a more brutal or more subtle way we will end up
staying on the side of the apparatus of heterosexuality. In other words,
the *dispositif* of trying to take that subject where their sexuality does
not take them. Sexuality is something so complex, so delicate, linked
to emotions, love, the relationship to the other... But beware, the transference is very powerful, and much more when combined with the fact
that this subject, especially if he could not form a community, suffers
all the pressure of this heteronormative *dispositif.* Then it is likely that
this subject wants to be what they are not, but they will *never* be what
they are not. They can get married, have children, they can lead a life
as if it were, they can even be happy in that life... but there is something
of their truth that is going to be left out all the time and that most likely
somehow, for better or worse, will burst in. What is inscribed in the flesh
is indelible.

P: And what do you think of this point that you note about sexuality in
adolescence, as something to which you have to open your ear a little?

J: Taking the example you gave, I don't know if your patient was a teenager...

P: No, neither of them were teens...

J: But it clearly seems to me that there, in adolescence, is the point where *you
cannot be neutral.* I believe that as an analyst, at that point... it seems
to me that it is not a question of interpretation, that it is a question of
constituting oneself as an Other that allows this subject... to help him
to perceive that these relations of power exist and that they have to take
a position on them. That is not something natural. One as an analyst
has to intervene in such a way that that subject can perceive all that
Foucault taught us. That *this subject* can perceive it, because their life is
at stake in that. Live one way or another. So the analyst has to intervene
in such a way as to denature sexuality. May they de-pathologize their
way of loving, their way of feeling, their way of desiring. If you *don't do
that,* I think it's going to be pathologized, because the whole environment goes that way. It is a bit different when someone has already made
a community, because there they already have other references that are
very important. So, there it is likely that one has less work – in addition
to what gay kids are like now, who really have a very interesting head –
because perhaps these devices have already been perceived, because
they opened up to those relations. For that, not to mention the blessing
that the internet is for lesbian, gay, trans teenagers, being able to talk
with others, share experiences, it is a difference... It is tremendous, it is
day and night!

M: It is good to speak up and be able to talk with others.

J: Absolutely, it is necessary. *That already destabilizes the power relations, once you can talk...* Did you see when the siblings start talking to each other about their parents? They start talking to each other about their parents to criticize them, that is a big step in life. Well this would be a bit equivalent. When they start talking to each other and share each other's experiences and feelings, they no longer feel that what is happening to them is tremendous and a disaster which happens to her or to him alone. They can start talking in community, and well, that makes a huge difference.

P: Yes, you make me think that there is no abstinence like silence on the points where you can only take a position as a person. Politically there is no way not to have a position. That "I don't like politics" is already a stance.

J: It is a political stance, of course, generally conservative, the conservative vision is "I am apolitical".

P: It may not be necessary because, like the first example, the analysand already comes knowing there is a community which provides support...

J: Totally.

P: In that case I have nothing to say because it does not add or take away.

J: But also, starting from this base, *psychoanalysis is not neutral*, that is, psychoanalysis looks for certain aims. We are not neutral from the start. *Betting on desire is political.* The church has other points of view and it is valid. It is not the one *I choose*, but it is a policy that many people are comfortable with. Saying "I am going to listen to you, and based on what I am going to hear I am going to intervene to interpret your desire"... that is not neutral at all. Neutrality should be well located. Neutrality is "I'm not going to ask you to be what I want you to be". There is neutrality there. "I will not try to make you make my choice, I will try to let you make your choice". And there one refrains from "I think you should separate". It is your problem if you would like them to separate, as an analyst, you have to be able to follow the path of the patient. Or anyhow, point out... target their anxiety, to the contradictions in what they are saying. In this case *there is* neutrality. But in other cases neutrality is complicated. Speaking of other sexualities: if you are neutral, you are on the side of the heterosexuality *dispositif.* As you said, in the first case of yours, no intervention was necessary, but in the second case it was.

P: Yes, after I formed this group in Ameghino, where we began to exchange readings among ourselves, we said: "let's think about why *trans* patients do not come, and see what we can do about it..."

J: But there was already some concern regarding this... There were people who asked themselves that question.

Gender studies and psychoanalysis: neither exclusive, nor entirely in agreement

P: The readings it produced... you know that the feeling that I had when I started reading Butler, Anne Fausto Sterling... reading these texts came to me as an almost naive surprise: how can it be that we, analysts, are not there, in large quantities, conversing with gender studies? Because, you know what came to my mind? It was: *psychoanalysis has no future outside of this conversation, because they have the truth on sexuality and we no longer do.*

J: Everything you are saying is what I have been saying for a long time, we completely agree. The same thing happens to me, it catches my attention... having such an interesting discourse... I would even tell you: *we don't have to agree on everything.* But in all this enormous proliferation of discourses on sexuality there are ideas so fabulous and so different from the canonical ideas of psychoanalysis. Why don't we listen to them? Why aren't we more open to these ideas? Why not? My mind has changed so much... and I think for the better. *Although, if you open up your mind, you have to question a few things, and there are people who love that, but there are people who do not want to question what is established, because as soon as you question it... you are already castrating the father.* You know how there is a certain Lacanism, I do not know if you have that impression, that speaks as if all the knowledge was already in Lacan's seminars and writings and that if you take a long, long, long time... you will finally acquire it some day, that "someday" that never comes, and meanwhile you keep reading, or feeling that you should be reading Lacan over and over again, and life goes on, but you don't realize it.

P: Yes, totally, that attitude is very common, it seems to me.

J: That is very sad, it is very common and it is like that Lacanism *does not want it to be otherwise.*

P: It seems that (if you open that dialogue) you have to give input to politics, to think about politics and power relations. Because somehow it becomes something constitutive and, I think, that there is also a sector in psychoanalysis that thinks politics could be on the outside. Reading Butler impressed me a lot, I don't know if you have it in mind, there is a book called *The Psychic life of Power*, where there is an idea that she presents, reading Freud, which is the idea of *gender melancholy* and that, as I understood, presents the idea that our culture proposes us not only to have to necessarily gender ourselves in *one* way and orient our sexuality according to *one* way, but also that since it is forbidden to love the same gender, therefore the love that has existed for the parent of the same gender cannot be mourned. She thinks about it especially for heterosexuality: that a mourning becomes impossible because I *could never have wanted* to love the same gender...

J: In other words, I could not have wanted to love the one who is forbidden to love...

P: That it has nothing to do with the idea of the mourning achieved, but with the impossibility of mourning due to the consequences of this generic formatting. And, by proposing it like this, in some way she is also questioning if we necessarily need gender as it is proposed to constitute ourselves as subjects.

The different ways of jouissance, do they oppose or enhance each other?

J: I think that sometimes there are tremendous demands based on how gender is proposed. Including the requirement, especially for the male, of exclusivity: "you should only enjoy things in a manly way". There was an article[25]... it caught my attention so much that I said, how can we not jump to draw conclusions from this? It is an article that touches upon a point, I would almost say uncomfortable, comical, or inelegant, but so interesting... I think the article is from Pavlovsky. He recounted an experience - I don't remember in which hospital - of a guy who cured male impotence. But it seems that he cured it for real. And you know how difficult it is to resolve the issue of sexual impotence at times. I am going to tell you as I remember it, surely I am misquoting it, because I read it a long time ago. I still have it on file, because I said "I have to save this". It is about a urologist who had invented a very simple method to cure impotence... I think he would make an appointment with the partner or the wife of the man who had the problem and gave them the solution: it was a small bottle of Vaseline, and he said to the woman "while you guys are having sex, stick a finger up his ass". And you know what? It worked. As if I were saying to you: if the guy could include some of the feminine jouissance, the masculine jouissance was much better. It's crazy, right? How the guy's ass seems to be untouchable, and avoiding it seems like a cornerstone of culture... yet that experience proves that things work the opposite of how it is believed. *It was not that one canceled the other out but that one enhanced the other.* Apparently, they fired that doctor, the patriarchy could not bear that this was happening. Which is quite consistent with the patriarchy, which is partly based on the father's ass being untouchable, basically.

P: You make me think of two things: one is something that my brother-in-law once told me (we were talking about sexuality) put into a football phrase: *"a phalanx is not a foul"*, it is allowed. (laughs) And on the other hand, Silvia Bleichmar's book *Paradojas de la sexualidad masculina*.

J: Ah, that's a very brave book.

P: That touches on that issue, of even how the least defensive heterosexuality that one can think of is armed with a passage and an elaboration of the homosexual bond.

We don't want to be subjects all the time

J: I think it goes even further, I think the *cornerstone of masculinity is based on a homosexual scene, which is the scene of the man receiving the father's phallus.* In part, masculinity has such a hard time dealing with homosexuality, but at the same time it is dealing with it all the time, because it is intrinsic to it. So are there better ways to solve it?

Before saying goodbye, I want to touch on a point that seems important to me... . Excuse me, but I have to go. It's on this: just as I think we can learn a lot from all these studies: *gay studies*, from *queer* theory, from gender studies... we have a lot to contribute as well. Because there is a dimension – and in this area I do believe that psychoanalysis is impeccable – which is the dimension of the object. Many of these studies, in my opinion, are based on the idea that one *wants to be a subject all the time*[26]... and that is where, for me, the spirit of psychoanalysis comes in, which is to bring a part of evil (so called, seen from, obviously, the phallic position) that one of the forms evil can take is *the jouissance of the object.*[27] I wouldn't even say "it's okay"... I don't know, because part of the fun is that it's wrong. *But there is that other part of the jouissance that has to do with losing, that has to do with submitting oneself, but submitting not because the other submits you against your will, but with the desire to... which has to do with the feminine... and that part, let's say, is not politically correct, but the clinic all the time teaches you that that part exists.* And it doesn't seem to me that the best solution is to deny it, to say "we want to be subjects all the time". It's not true, we don't want to be subjects all the time. We also want to be in the position of the object, some more, others less, in general people tend to be more in one position or another, but there is that jouissance of the place of the object. According to Tiresias, you know, it is much greater than the subject's jouissance. The feminine jouissance, he says, if there are ten parts of jouissance, nine are feminine. Tiresias was obviously gay, it's very clear (laughs). He was gay but versatile. He tried both sides and said "no, this one is better..." (laughs).

P: I thought that if psychoanalysis gives rise to that, it is because, in this way, it also enables it to be part of a shared game and not necessarily in a suffering way.

J: It's totally in a joyous way, I think, in the erotic scene. It is: *let's play this role of the object. Obviously that role, like everything important in life, is dangerous.* Because that also could end in "Ni una menos",[28] it also could end in a woman, a transvestite or a gay kid beaten or killed. But to believe that this dimension exists only by involuntary submission and that there is no desire... is a lie. This dimension exists because there is jouissance on that side, it is a jouissance of the subject, but occupying the role of an object. There is the paradox, and the difficulty.

P: It over-victimizes the victim, I think.

J: Sure, and that area is super delicate. *We even touch* – and that is the place of psychoanalysis – *topics that can hardly be talked about*. Because when you speak on these topics they will always want to put words in your mouth and claim you said things you did not say. You're not saying it's okay to beat the shit out of your wife. But if you like some spankings in the erotic scene, enjoy it. Or if, to go to more extreme experiences, if your way of living eroticism is through sado-masochism, well, it is not because you are sick, it is that erotic jouissance can also take that form. And as analysts, let's not pathologize that part of jouissance that has to do with the object, the bad part, the cursed part, as Bataille called it. The part that threatens narcissism.

The concepts do not only want to be respected

M: It is interesting because you always stop at an intermediate point of the two speeches and you leave both incomplete. This technique of reading, research, and use of concepts is interesting...

J: I like that, the concepts are there to help change lives. I don't care for glamorous and empty concepts, I like useful concepts. The concepts that are not useful for thinking and to change something in life are not so interesting to me. For me, many of these ideas changed my life. *My life*. And I hope they help me make changes in the lives of others. If one is going into an analysis to leave the same as when they entered, what was this whole process for? It doesn't make sense, it's to change something ...

I thank you infinitely, but I have to go...

M: We thank you, Jorge.

P: Thanks to you, Jorge.

J: A pleasure.

Notes

1 Manuel Murillo, professor and researcher at the UBA School of Psychology, is the author of ¿Qué son los tres registros? *Genealogía de una hipótesis de J. Lacan (2017) and ¿Qué es la época? Psicoanálisis, historia y subjetividad (2018)*.

2 Pablo Tajman is a clinical psychologist, he is interested in various theorizations, techniques, and devices of psychoanalysis and related disciplines. He is the coordinator of the Interdisciplinary Residency of the "Dr. Ángel Bo" Health Center and a member of Groups of the Mental Health Center No 3 "Dr. A. Ameghino".

3 An expression in Spanish that means "you can't have too much of a good thing".

4 https://psicoanalisisynopsicoanalisis.com/.

5 I am referring to Manuel's book on Lacan's three registers.

6 I thank Olga Pilnik who was the first to call my attention to this. (Jorge).

7 The video Edipo gay, by the YouTube channel Asociación Libre, of Matías Tavil, can be seen here: https://www.youtube.com/watch?v=r_wa139T20A&t=18s.

8 6 *Oedipus gay*, in this book.

 9 Centro Ameghino is a hospital in Buenos Aires, Argentina. It was founded in 1948 by the Ministry of Health, and was initially designated as the "Institute of Applied Psychopathology".

10 Regarding this, I want to clarify two things: first, I am referring to reading the analyst's desire beyond his role as analyst, not his desire as an analyst, but the desires that in principle should remain outside the experience of analysis (such as example Freud's desire that Ferenczi be his "vizier and secret paladin"), but they *always* "sneak in", since no one can fulfill their "pure" role. Second, it is not lost on me that the analyst *also* lends themselves so that the analysand projects their relation to the desire of their primary Others. (Jorge).

11 The writing of this book is the most substantial part, the product and also the testimony of the arduous journey I had to make after the fall of the transference in order to finish my analysis; *Gay & Lesbian studies* and queer theory were my Groddeck, my other Other that allowed me to elaborate what, for the reasons that I develop in this same book, I had not found a place in three different analyses.

12 It is at this time that Freud wrote, in a letter to Ferenczi, a phrase that became famous: "I have succeeded where the paranoid [Fliess] fails". (Jorge).

13 Elizabeth Severn. (Jorge).

14 In relation to this point, see Ferenczi, S. (1995) *The Clinical Diary of Sándor Ferenczi*, Harvard University Press.

15 El análisis original, in Mannoni, Octave, La otra escena, Claves de lo imaginario, Amorrortu editores, Buenos Aires, 1979 (No translation to English).

16 [A celebration of a goal is heard everywhere, we continue talking as if nothing had happened].

17 Ricardo Rodulfo is a prestigious Argentine analyst and a specialist in child psychoanalysis.

18 Regarding this point, I emphatically recommend the text by Arnold L. Davidson *The emergence of sexuality*, Harvard University Press, Cambridge Massachusetts, London England 2001. (Jorge).

19 In the heat of the conversation I forgot at least one other idea that is original to Freud and tremendously powerful in its consequences: that of the structurally incestuous character of infantile sexuality and its importance for adult sexuality. (Jorge).

20 In the inter-team group on gender and diversity of the Mental Health Center No. 3, Dr. A. Ameghino.

21 That it is not disconnected from the political position and the personal position of the analyst. (Pablo).

22 What place is there in the proposal of Elementary Structures of Kinship for homosexuality?

23 I am not unaware of intersex, although I will not discuss it here.

24 Of course, what can be done (and is in progress) is to redefine what is feminine, what is masculine, and what does not fit into those categories.

25 *La mejor cura para la impotencia sexual*, by Eduardo "Tato" Pavlovsky. It can be read at http://www.pagina12.com.ar/diario/psicologia/9-231381-2013-10-17.html (Jorge).

26 In those studies, if one occupies the role of an object, it is in the form of the victim. Victim of misogynistic violence, or homophobic, or transphobic, etc. That it is a totally real and fundamental dimension, but it does not exhaust the question of the object and the jouissance.

27 See *On the political incorrectness of eroticism*, in this book.

28 "Not one [woman] less" is a Latin American fourth-wave grassroots feminist movement, which started in Argentina and has spread across several Latin American countries, that campaigns against gender-based violence.

Bibliography

Bleichmar, S. (2006). *Paradojas de la sexualidad masculina.* Buenos Aires: Paidós.

Ferenczi, S. (1995). *The clinical diary of Sándor Ferenczi.* Cambridge, MA and London: Harvard University Press.

Ferenczi, S. (2018). *Final contributions to the problems and methods of psycho-analysis.* New York, NY and London: Routledge.

Freud, S. (1964). *The standard edition of the complete psychological works of Sigmund Freud, Volume XXIII (1937–1939).* London: The Hogarth Press.

Mannoni, O. (1979). *La otra escena, Claves de lo imaginario.* Buenos Aires: Amorrortu Editores.

Epilogue

This epilogue is a new version of the speech I gave at the book presentation at the Universidad de Buenos Aires, in April 2019. I decided to keep some of the colloquial language.

Speaking up

There are many ways to describe how an analysis works. None will be exhaustive, each one will emphasize an aspect of that complex process that is an analysis. Defining an analysis as the long and difficult process of losing the fear of speaking may be too limited. Although, I dare to say that it is a description that covers an essential point and that is deeper than it seems at first glance. The *act* of speaking up has far-reaching consequences. Like any act, once produced, is irreversible, it establishes a before and after, and is transformative. It transforms the subject who speaks up and uses the power of speech, while, to some extent, micro or macro, transforming the world.

Since we are going to talk about gayness, let us say that a person's life is not the same before or after that act of speaking up and coming out of the closet. Life around them is not the same either. Suppose a family wants to pretend that nothing changed after one of its members came out of the closet. This is impossible, even if the family denies it, that act of speaking up cannot be erased.[1] That is on the micro scale, on the macro scale, for example, when Freud published *The Interpretation of Dreams*, he changed the course of history. Brilliant as the textbook about child neurology which Freud wrote and published around the same time was, that would not be "speaking up" in the meaning that I am giving it at the moment. What I say is evident in that many of you may not have been aware of the existence of that textbook, but surely no one here is unaware of the existence of *The Interpretation of Dreams*, whether you have read it or not. In the sense that I am giving it now, speaking up is to say something new (sometimes new for the subject, sometimes new for the world), something that is transgressive and creative.

What happens when someone's word is not accepted? Either a part of that subject dies, or else they must continue insisting on making themselves

DOI: 10.4324/9781003252160-12

heard. Given the radical dependence of the subject on the Other, the act of speaking up requires, on the part of the person or persons who embody the place of the Other, what we could call *listening*, giving that word in this context the meaning of an opening toward the other as an other, an ability to allow oneself to be questioned, and (here the Lacanians are going to kill me) something that I would call compassion, the ability to try to put oneself in the other's place.[2] The subtle interplay between speaking and listening is not always possible, it does not depend only on the will of the subject or the benevolence of the Other, it depends very strongly on something that I discuss thoroughly in the book, power relations. If for centuries, literally, no one publicly claimed gayness, it is clearly not because there were neither desires nor acts of those who would later be called "homosexuals", it is because the state of power relations did not allow even considering doing so.

However, a historical moment occurred, which we can place in the last decades of the nineteenth century, in which for the first time in many centuries, power relations allowed "homosexuality" to speak up in the first person to claim their right to exist legitimately. Including, its joy, and enjoyment, and sorrows, and way of loving, and so on. Psychoanalysis, born of Freud's desire to hear the word that doctors did not want or could not hear, remains surprisingly deaf to "homosexuality" *as an enunciative act*,[3] and leaves it on the side of pathology or "perversion". Despite Freud's undoubted vocation to listen, the state of power relations did not allow him to finish moving away from the limitations imposed by the heteronormative regime. On this point, as I discuss in the book, he sticks to the position of psychiatry of his time.

I think it is an understatement to say that psychoanalysis in general has spoken *of* homosexuals and not *with* homosexuals,[4] because even in the second case, where "homosexuals" would have a status of subjects, the field of psychoanalysis is established as a heterosexual field, or at most neutral: we, the psychoanalysts, speak with them, the "homosexuals". Although in these issues, there is no neutrality, just as no one is outside power relations, nobody is outside libidinal relations, and nobody speaks from a place purified of Eros. "We" analysts, includes, of course, many psychoanalysts who are "homosexual", though most are sadly closeted. That is why I believe that, if we want to reverse this situation, the main responsibility lies with psychoanalysts who "are"[5] also gay, or lesbian, or trans, or any other of what are called dissident sexualities.[6] I say "also" because I do not think anyone is gay or trans as a psychoanalyst, I do not think there is a gay listener and a straight one, a trans and a cis one. There are people who are sensitive to the subjectivity of the other, and others who are not. A capacity that is completely independent of how you enjoy yourself sexually. Of course, it is not easy at all to define what it means to "be gay", and here is where the problem of identity lies, about which psychoanalysis has very interesting things to say. I consider it fundamental that, we psychoanalysts whose sexuality does not respond to heterosexuality (in the genital sense, of course – Eros always implies an encounter with the hetero... of each subject), do not allow psychoanalysis to establish itself as a field of production of heterosexual or "neutral" knowledge. Make no mistake, in the logic of heteronormativity, neutral means normal, it means heterosexual. I am convinced that it can only be truly affirmed that psychoanalysis is not a heteronormative *dispositif* when psychoanalysts who are not heterosexual do not have to remain in the closet in psychoanalytic institutions, and when the enunciation of theoretical production is not made from a supposed heterosexuality, a libidinal neutrality that is nothing other than the supposedly nonexistent heteronormativity of psychoanalysis.

Do not think that it is easy for me to be here, saying all these things, in front of all of you. Maybe it is now, but it certainly was not easy to get to this point, to this subjective position, which is at the same time, inevitably, a political position (here the saying the personal is political applies). It is a step that is barely hinted at in the book I am presenting.[7] Although, from what Eve Kosofsky Sedgwick calls the epistemology of the closet, it is something that is going to be (correctly) read in the very act of the publication of the book. Easier put: it is unlikely that a heterosexual analyst would have written this book. It is a step that friends who care about me advised me not to take at the time of editing and publishing the first edition of this book; and in any case, I do not know if I would have been more explicit at that time. Although, the very publication of the book has had an effect on the author, and almost inevitably leads me to take this stance.

The act of speaking up is woven into a complex way in the book. It begins with the difficulties to solve my own analysis, which goes through three analyses. I would say that while many important aspects of the neurosis were being resolved, there was little place for something in my own words. If a piece of my own words did not find a place in *any* analysis, it seemed unlikely that it was (as many times has been argued to me) a problem of each individual analyst. When I was able to take enough critical distance to *think*, I concluded that I had run into a problem in psychoanalytic theory itself. I do not know how I would have been able to finish my own analysis, or if I would have even managed to finish it, if I had not come across lesbian and gay studies, which are, in turn, the transposition to the academic level of the gay liberation movement's act of speaking up. The feeling of freedom was immense, I felt as if for the first time in my life (or at least since puberty) I was breathing fresh air. For that, too, my gratitude was immense. I remember a conversation with my last analyst in which I heard myself saying that if I had to choose between a discourse that gave me space and another that did not, I had no doubt what my choice would be. My departure began from a certain way of thinking on psychoanalysis that left me outside and so did my search for new horizons to inhabit.

I remember a text by Leo Bersani (*Shame on you*[8]) that interested me so much that I took the trouble to translate it. After a couple of reads I realized that the hypotheses of the text did not matter so much to me, what caused me to translate it was the enunciative position. An intellectual, whose production was interesting to me, spoke, *as a gay man*, on issues of gayness, and furthermore, he was not complacent with the gay community itself, to which he pointed out its own contradictions. I had never read anything like it in psychoanalytic literature. Leo Bersani's enunciative position had a much stronger subjective effect on me than what he said. Something similar happened with my book, which is what I most desired. It can make many mistakes, its hypothesis can be completely questionable, rectifiable, and refutable. It does not mean that as an enunciative act it has not produced effects, because the book revealed something that was kept in silence (homophobia in the closet) and needed to be said, and at least was necessary for many people who felt the weight and damage of the heteronormativity of psychoanalysis.

I think that if the book had a certain repercussion it is because in the field of psychoanalysis it is speaking up to posit something that many people needed to hear. Of course, there are those who would prefer that the book did not exist (there were even those who considered it *scandalous* that it was published), but still, regardless of the merits or defects of the book, they cannot ignore it completely. The book takes the baton in the field of psychoanalysis of a much larger and more complex process of speaking up, of which I offer a few minimal brush strokes in the book itself. I speak up because others spoke up. That is why the book is also dedicated to the gay liberation movement: it is an acknowledgment of the debt I owe to those who came before me.

Repercussions

The publication of *Oedipus Gay*[9] generated something new: readers. In the presentation, which took place when it was published, I said that now the book was a little less mine and that they would be the ones who would tell me, in a certain sense, what I had written. Then those answers came. I want to highlight some of the ones that I especially appreciate because they are the ones that prove that "a letter always arrives at its destination"[10] (Lacan, 2002, p. 30) to gay psychoanalysts or psychology students, who find in the book something they needed, something in which they recognize themselves and that to some extent, relieves them. Their words bring me joy and honor me, although that is not why I want to share them, but because they seem to ratify some of the hypotheses of the book, against the disavowal of so much hegemonic psychoanalysis. For the purposes of this epilogue, I choose two.

Rodrigo Civetta (29 years old) introduces himself as follows: *My name is Rodrigo Civetta, I am a psychoanalyst, gay, and from Rosario. I have been living in San Martín de los Andes for a year and a half and I came across your book "Gay Oedipus" by chance. I have been searching (since I was a student) for psychoanalytic theoretical productions beyond the heteronormative ballast that, at times, pathologizes sexualities.* Here a generational difference appears: he could look for that type of production, in a world in which, for example, the word *heteronormative* exists. When I was myself a student at this college, the world was much more immersed in heteronormativity, which for that very reason was so invisible that it did not even have a name. Rodrigo continues: *I am still reading your book and I found your positions and productions interesting. And above all, relieved in terms of being able to think "oh well, what happened to me since I started reading psychoanalysis is not so crazy, I'm not alone in this".* Why is Rodrigo relieved, just like me when I came across lesbian and gay studies? Surely when he perceived and pointed out that "heteronormative and pathologizing ballast of sexualities" in the transmission of psychoanalysis, he must have found himself denied by many of his professors. As you know, if a person is denied their own perceptions (if a person is gay, I can tell from my own experience, heteronormativity is perceived, its violence is felt in the body, in things said and unsaid, in what is whispered; when not directly in heteronormative and homophobic comments), it is maddening. A person wonders if they are not crazy, and if they do not find any dialogue that gives rise to their own truth, they will most likely submit (and end up reproducing the same speech that oppresses them). I think the violence of that denial is even greater than the violence of heteronormativity, except that it is part of it.

To finish, I am going to quote a testimony that especially moves me. It is lengthy (still edited) but worth every word. His name is Seba Figueroa, he is also very young (24 years old[11]) and he writes to me about the book:

> *(...) I read it and I loved it. It actually invited me to think about myself, about myself in psychoanalysis, about what I wanted from psychoanalysis in light of my future. Personally, it was very moving. The truth is that I started an analysis because I was trying to process what my life was, which was in pieces after I came out of the closet. There I learned how interesting it is to accompany processes and singularities. Well, that face of psychoanalysis made me fall in love and I started psychology already thinking about being an analyst. But the psychoanalytic heteropatriarchy always weighed me down, often flaunted from the institutions and well, it made me doubt, it hurt me because despite the fact that I lack clinical practice (important detail) and much to learn, I feel that psychoanalysis is part of me.*

Rereading that founding text, *The Straight Mind*, by Monique Wittig, I found something that I had overlooked in other readings: the idea of a "science of oppression", or "science of our oppression". The "our" refers, of course, to all those who are not legitimized by the heterosexual mind. It is not a science *on* the oppressed subjects, but *by* them. Wittig takes this idea of a science of the oppressed from the phrase of a Romanian peasant in a public assembly, who in 1848 (not just any year in European history) posited: "Why do the gentlemen say it was not slavery, for we know it to have been slavery, this sorrow that we have sorrowed". (Wittig, 1992, p. 31) She claims that this "science of oppression" is something that "cannot be taken away from us", and I agree, except that I would add "once we reach it". If Wittig understands that by being oppressed, that science would immediately be counted on, I would disagree. The oppressed may be unaware of their oppression and still sustain it. I have done it myself for far too long. It would be interesting to investigate what are the ways that allow success in this science. I would say, in our psychoanalytic language, that it is necessary to have achieved, to some extent, the inconsistency of the Other, and in a Foucauldian key, it is necessary to have achieved a certain understanding of power relations. For this to be achieved it is necessary to be part of a community. Seba (as well as Rodrigo) does not doubt the existence of a "psychoanalytic heteropatriarchy, often flaunted from the institutions", it does not have to be explained to him, because he is equipped with the science of our oppression. He knows, therefore, that this heteropatriarchy is not just a theoretical problem, that it does damage. I understand that this science is something simple, something that needs to be achieved, developed, grown, questioned, and shared, but that basically consists of the certainty that those who are oppressed have that they are oppressed. "Why do psychoanalysts tell us that it is not heteronormativity, if we know that this oppression that oppresses us is heteronormativity?" I continue with Seba:

> *(…) now I see myself immersed in a more real, authentic, creative psycho-analysis … suddenly, when looking directly at the face of psychoanalysis that you propose (for me the only possible one since Freud and others…) I was able to project a future where I see myself as a psychoanalyst. You know when desire is constrained in a patient, when they want something but are always five cents too short? When they were about to obtain it, something happened. Well, that happened to me with psychoanalysis. I fell in love, I was passionate but … suddenly something about it appeared that seemed to leave me outside myself and close the door.*

At first, I was surprised when I read that Seba spoke of the "psychoanalysis that you propose". Am I perhaps proposing *another* psychoanalysis? I asked myself. Perhaps, to some extent, yes. One that does not leave him out, that does not close the door on him, that does not close it on me either. I also propose that this psychoanalysis is the same as always, that it recovers what is very much its essence and frees itself from at least one part of the ballast of the unthought. In this sense, my desire is to make it "more real, more authentic". Without a doubt I aspire to achieve a more creative psychoanalysis, above all, because the life of thought is in the possibility of not repeating dogmas endorsed by some authority, but at all times being able to think differently, always maintaining a critical disposition, even (or rather especially) toward those theories that make us fall in love.

> *Now I feel that, in the design of the psychoanalytic dispositif, Freud, (in his context) built a theory also designed for me and for many others. You know, I have only told my analyst that I think I studied Psychology*

because I had such a bad time with myself and my homosexuality, espe-
cially in adolescence, that I think I can do something for people like me,
not just homosexual people, but for all those who hated themselves, those
who wanted to be others, those who cried when they saw their secret love
slip away between fear and horror. How curious! I want to be a psycholo-
gist to cure that kid who still sometimes cries today, even though he does
not hate himself so much anymore…

Of course, we always want to be therapists (remember that etymologically
it is the one who cares, attends, and soothes) also to heal ourselves. As for
the ills of the soul, curing ourselves is always curing, at the same time, the
child we were.

You taught me that to be a good professional, teacher and psychoanalyst,
you do not have to pretend. You can be a fag and a psychoanalyst and it
is alright…
(…) before I came out of the closet, what happened to me in general
was that my homosexual desire constantly appeared and I tried to suf-
focate it, like saying "nothing is going on here" (…). My doubts arose
about what was expected of me as an analysand and a future gay analyst
and I suffocated them, I did not look at that because I knew that it put in
check a desire of mine that was very strong. What I mean is that through
your book I was able to give way to that desire for psychoanalysis (ana-
lyzing and analyzed) without the cost of leaving anyone out. Not even
myself.

Then you appeared … Here, in the original message, Seba adds some musical
notes, as if a bolero had slipped into the middle of the speech.

There was an act with your book. An instituting act that allows us to talk
about homosexuality and psychoanalysis without hesitation. (…) I mean,
with your book the gay analysts have a reading that goes far beyond the
official story. It is rather a story not told, that is veiled and it is the possi-
bility that analysts and analyzed can give effect to their two wishes, as is
our case. Our gay desire and our psychoanalytic desire.

I am perfectly aware of that tension between "homosexual desire" and the
analyst's desire, that distressing feeling one desire "put the other in check".
It cost me a lot of anxiety when I was myself studying at this college, in
which it was discussed whether a homosexual, supposedly a pervert, could
be a psychoanalyst.[12] The old discussion of 1920 continued in Buenos Aires
in the eighties. The context was much more oppressive than the one Seba
speaks of because there were no voices that helped to think otherwise, there
were no words that allowed another subjective position. Not there at least.
Although, Seba does not have it so easy in 2019 either.

If Seba says that my book taught him that "you can be a fag and a psychoanalyst and it is alright", that the book is an "instituting act that allows you to talk about homosexuality and psychoanalysis openly", it means that something is up, that there are still barriers, that the discourses and omissions, and with them the devices of power that anguished me in the eighties, that put in tension, as Seba says, my "gay desire" with my desire to be a psychoanalyst, are still valid in 2019. Otherwise the book would have been superfluous, it would not have taught him anything and it would not have instituted anything.

Then Seba says words that I dearly hope are true:

> *The instituting act of your book is psychoanalysis coming out of the closet. An alternative title could be "Oedipus Gay: Psychoanalysis Coming Out of the Closet". Taking the act of coming-out-of-the-closet as something that for the first time puts into play, before others, a veiled, suffocated, repressed desire. Right?*

An act of speaking up. There is not much to add, because Seba said everything that I would have wanted to tell you and everything that I wanted to be said. If at least for him the book occupied that instituting place, I already feel that it was worth having written it. Even better if it occupies that place for others.

Thank you very much.

Notes

1 This does not mean that trying to deny it does not have very heavy consequences.
2 I am not referring to compassion in the sense of enveloping the other in one's own narcissism to make one, or the idea that we are the same; but quite the opposite, an attempt to put oneself in the place of the other to the extent that it implies breaking the assumption of sameness. Compassion in this sense requires a renunciation of the narcissism of believing that one is the measure of all things.
3 Consequently, as a producer of knowledge.
4 That was the request of the incipient gay liberation movement to the psychiatrists of the American Psychiatric Association at the beginning of the process of removing homosexuality from the DSM.
5 Oh, the verb to be!
6 Will there be any sexuality that, in some way, is not dissident?
7 It was at that time the first edition of the book.
8 Bersani, L., Phillips, A. (2008), Intimacies, The University of Chicago Press, 31.
9 In the Spanish edition the title of the book was *Oedipus Gay*, and its subtitle was *Heteronormativity and Psychoanalysis*.
10 This is an allusion to Lacan's famous assertion in the article "Seminar on the Purloined Letter" of his Ecrits, "a letter always arrives at its destination" (Lacan, 1966, 41).
11 On the topics of this book, dialogue with young people is much easier for me than with colleagues of my generation.
12 At the end of this presentation, someone from the audience approached me to tell me "this university delayed me coming out of the closet for many years". I understood them perfectly.

Bibliography

Bersani, L., & Phillips, A. (2008). *Intimacies*. Chicago, IL and London: The University of Chicago Press.

Lacan, J. (2002). *Ecrits*. New York, NY and London: W. W. Norton & Company.

Wittig, M. (1992). *The straight mind*. Boston, MA: Beacon Press.

Index

Note: Page numbers followed by "n" denote endnotes.

For Product Safety Concerns and Information please contact our EU
representative GPSR@taylorandfrancis.com
Taylor & Francis Verlag GmbH, Kaufingerstraße 24, 80331 München, Germany